BITTERSWEET PASSAGE

PASSAGE

—

REDRESS
and the Japanese
Canadian Experience

Maryka Omatsu

between the lines

Copyright © Maryka Omatsu, 1992
Published by Between The Lines
      394 Euclid Avenue
      Toronto, Ontario
      M6G 2S9 Canada

Front cover illustration by Aiko Suzuki
Cover design by Counterpunch
Backcover photograph by Frank Cunningham
Typeset by Adams and Hamilton, Toronto
Printed in Canada

Between The Lines gratefully acknowledges the financial contribution to the
publication of this book from the Heritage Cultures and Languages Program of
Multiculturalism and Citizenship Canada.

The following copyright holders have granted permission to reprint material:
Roger Bowen, *Rebellion and Democracy in Meiji Japan: A Study of Commoners in
the Popular Rights Movement*, copyright © 1980, The Regents of the University of
California. Roy Miki, editor and Wes Fujiwara, executor, *This Is My Own: Letters
to Wes & Other Writings on Japanese Canadians, 1941-1948*, by Muriel Kitagawa,
copyright © 1985, the authors. Kazuo Ito, *Issei: A History of Japanese Immigrants in
North America*, translated by S. Nakamura and J. Gerard, copyright © Japanese
Community Service, Seattle, Washington, 1973. All attempts made to locate the
publisher were fruitless. *The Book of Five Rings* by Miyamoto Musashi, copyright
© 1982 by Bantam, a division of Bantam Doubleday Dell Publishing Group, Inc.
Takeo Ujo Nakano, translation by Leatrice Nakano Willson, for the tanka that
appears at the beginning of chapter one. Takeo Ujo Nakano with Leatrice
Nakano Willson for the tanka that begins chapter two and appears in *Within the
Barbed Wire Fence*, copyright © 1980, University of Toronto Press.

Between The Lines gratefully acknowledges the financial support of the Canada
Council, the Ontario Arts Council, and the Ontario Ministry of Culture and
Communications, through the Ontario Publishing Centre.

CANADIAN CATALOGUING IN PUBLICATION DATA

Omatsu, Maryka, 1949-
    Bittersweet passage

Includes index.

ISBN 0-921284-57-8 (bound) ISBN 0-921284-58-6 (pbk.)

1. Japanese Canadians – Evacuation and relocation, 1942-1945.*
2. World War, 1939-1945 – Reparations. I. Title.

FC106.J3O63 1992 971'.00495 C92-093717-9
F1035.J3O63 1992

Dedicated to the issei, nisei, and sansei
who fought for justice against great odds

to my parents, Satsuko and Denno Omatsu,

and to my husband, Frank Cunningham

GLOSSARY

issei	first generation Japanese Canadian (*sei* means "generation")
nisei	second generation
sansei	third generation
yonsei	fourth generation
gosei	fifth generation
nihonjin	Japanese (*jin* means "person")
hakujin	white person
gaijin	foreigner
yamato-damashii	warrior and/or harmony spirit
shikataga-nai	fatalistic resignation
sodan-kai	group to reach consensus
ganbari	resistance

Contents

❀ | Preface and Acknowledgements

THE WINNING OF redress restored honour to my community. For Japanese Canadians, it was our sweetest moment, and for all Canadians it marks one of the most significant civil rights victories in the history of this country. I feel extremely fortunate to have been a participant in this struggle and I remain empowered by our triumph.

After the public announcement in September, 1988, I spent over two years researching, interviewing, writing, and thinking about the seminal event in my life. This book is a distillation of my thoughts as an activist and a lawyer. As a personal account of the redress years, it reflects my biases and experiences, which were largely confined to the Toronto area.

My most profound gratitude for our success must go to the unsung heroes in the National Association of Japanese Canadians who helped make it possible and to those Canadians who supported our cause.

For their assistance in the writing of this book, I am especially indebted to: Susan Crean, Frank Cunningham, Andrew Danson, Jock

Ferguson, Shin Imai, Bryce Kanbara, Joy Kogawa, Audrey Kobayashi, Andrea Margles, Art Miki, Jesse Nishihata, Roger Obata, Erna Paris, Marlene Nourbese Philip, Andrew Ranachan, Rick Salutin, Rick Shiomi, and Ann Gomer Sunahara. I also want to thank Aiko Suzuki for reading and commenting on a draft of my book, and for the cover illustration.

I am also very appreciative of all those people who allowed me to share their lives, however briefly. The list is too lengthy for me to mention them individually, but you will recognize your contributions on every page of my book.

Thanks must go to my agent Lee Davis Creal of the Lucinda Vardey Agency, for her consistent support, to my excellent editor Robert Clarke, and to the members of the Between The Lines collective.

I am grateful to Ken Adachi for writing his book, *The Enemy That Never Was*, to Ann Gomer Sunahara for her book, *The Politics of Racism: The Uprooting of Japanese Canadians During the Second World War*, and to Roy Miki and Cassandra Kobayashi for their book, *Justice In Our Time: The Japanese Canadian Redress Settlement*. Finally, however, none of these people is responsible for any errors or omissions that may have occurred in the text, or for my interpretations. These are, of course, my responsibility.

As a final note of appreciation, I wish to acknowledge the generosity of the Canada Council Arts Awards program, the Ontario Arts Council, and the Japanese Canadian Redress Foundation for their financial contributions.

❀ | Foreword
by Edward Broadbent

AT ONE POINT in this remarkable book Maryka Omatsu says of her Canadian ancestors: "Transplanted adventurous peasants from a feudal island, we helped to clear the forests, to harvest the seas, and to develop a virgin country." With one exception, the word "feudal," I could have written the same sentence. Maryka Omatsu and I are both third-generation Canadians. Her ancestors and mine did indeed do all that she notes. However, unlike her, I never picked up my father's wallet following his death to find carefully preserved a government-issued card that included a photo and a thumb print and a description of him as an "enemy alien." The difference is that her Canadian ancestors came from Japan and mine came from the British Isles.

In good measure this book is about what flows from such accidents of birth. In part it tells the sad story about the vile treatment of one group of human beings by another. But it is also about how the Japanese Canadian community came together behind new leadership in the 1980s to compel by force of argument and documentation of fact the Canadian government to redress that terrible injustice.

In the course of reading we discover that the persecution of twenty-two thousand innocent Japanese Canadians in the 1940s had nothing to do with the necessities of war but instead was the result of racism and political expediency. Although Prime Minister Mackenzie King's Liberal government made the decision in spite of evidence provided by the RCMP and the defence department that showed it was unwarranted, it did so in the confident belief that existing racism aimed at the "yellow peril" would make such an act more than merely acceptable. The Canadian government's decision resulted in the seizure of property, forced migration, and the denial of other fundamental rights to men, women, and children born in Canada whose only "crime" was that their ancestors came from Japan. It was not a nice moment in our history.

Maryka Omatsu's book does not concentrate on the circumstances or details of the decision, which have already been discussed by others. Rather her emphasis is on the aftermath of the 1940s persecution and in particular on the dramatically successful campaign to obtain redress for the injustice.

If there were few in the broader Canadian community who appeared with honour during this incident almost five decades ago, it is encouraging to read of what can reasonably be described as a transformation in opinion by the 1980s. It was this transformation that led to Prime Minister Mulroney's announcement of September 22, 1988, in the House of Commons of the formal apology of Parliament to Japanese Canadians and the provision of $21,000 to each of the survivors.

While it is evident that Mulroney must be given praise for doing what Pierre Trudeau had explicitly refused to do when he was prime minister (on the specious grounds that you cannot remake history), the ultimate credit for redress must be given to the small band of "nisei" and "sansei," the second and third generation of Japanese Canadians, whose determined leadership at every stage made this decision possible.

A small group under the leadership of Art Miki, who has been appropriately described as " honest, stubborn, a consensus builder," first won a major battle within the Japanese Canadian community and then went on in an imaginative and courageous struggle to mobilize public opinion.

Without this leadership from justice-driven nisei and sansei, redress would not have occurred. Elderly Japanese Canadians, innocent victims who have done so much for our country and who now can die in peace with their honour restored, owe them a great deal. I am sure the author's mother, who participated in her first political demonstration on Parliament Hill at the age of seventy-five, would strongly agree. However, we non-Japanese Canadians must also thank this dedicated group. For without their work our record would remain dismally unmodified. You cannot remake history but you can and must redress a great injustice.

There are many groups, individuals, and institutions who emerge honourably in this important story. Working-class Hamiltonians supported the redress petition campaign. Many ethnic groups throughout the country joined in. The municipal councils of Toronto, Vancouver, and Lethbridge made important decisions at the right time. The editorial boards of *The Globe and Mail* and *The Toronto Star,* and Canadian journalists in general, are singled out for praise. The head of the national veterans' association refused to support a resolution against redress, speaking accurately when he said such a resolution "would disgrace its own membership: the veterans sweat blood to protect innocent people." When I read these words, I thought of a favourite uncle who died from wounds received on a distant beach in the war against Nazism.

There are others who emerge much less honourably, notably the Ontario Command of the Royal Canadian Legion who voted to oppose redress. There is also a disturbing reference to Canada's organized women's movement whom Omatsu describes as being non-co-operative. Like the business community in general, she says they were indifferent to their cause.

Bittersweet Passage is a fine book that should be put on required reading lists for students throughout Canada. No better introduction to what human rights are all about can be found. I say this not only because it vividly and honestly describes a terrible violation of human rights but also because in a very real sense one can see the virtues of our democratic history: a courageous, tough-minded group, armed with nothing but facts and a determination for justice, was able to make a difference. We will never be able to undo the harm inflicted on Maryka Omatsu's father who, like so many, many others, was compelled to leave his roots in his beloved

British Columbia for which he yearned "with the longing of a lost love." But we can learn from the struggle of his children's generation. We must learn that a struggle must continually be waged against racism and its horrible consequences, which are always felt in the daily lives of quite particular human beings.

Signing the Redress agreement in Ottawa, September 22, 1988, Prime Minister Brian Mulroney and NAJC *President Art Miki.*

BITTERSWEET
PASSAGE

1 | The End

Our dark cloud of a half century dissipated
The fairest day
In Japanese-Canadian history
Dawns.
Our joy is unsurpassable.

– Tanka by Takeo Ujo Nakano to commemorate the
Japanese Canadian redress settlement, September 22,
1988. Translation by Leatrice Nakano Willson

IN MID-SEPTEMBER 1988 I received a long-awaited phone call after weeks of feeling as though I'd been suspended from the ceiling by fish hooks. Even then I wasn't quite ready for what Art Miki said, in his calm, organized manner. "Maryka? Come to Ottawa for September twenty-second. It's still top secret, so don't breathe a word of this, but our deal has got the prime minister's go ahead."

I sat down on a kitchen chair, weak-kneed from a heady mixture of relief and excitement. Finally, Brian Mulroney had ratified an agreement that the National Association of Japanese Canadians had been pursuing for over four years.

We had been waiting for the green light from the prime minister since August 27, when the NAJC negotiators had wound up a successful hush-hush meeting at the Ritz-Carlton Hotel in Montreal. Three days earlier seven of us had been ushered into the hotel's fancy Chambre de Conseil: Art Miki, the NAJC's president and a Winnipeg school principal;

Audrey Kobayashi, a Montreal professor; Cassandra Kobayashi, a Vancouver lawyer; Roy Miki, Art's brother and a Vancouver professor; Roger Obata, a retired businessman from Toronto; and myself, a Toronto lawyer. Don Rosenbloom, an NAJC legal advisor, was also with us.

For years, the NAJC's representatives had been running into roadblock after roadblock in our attempts to win redress for the wartime wrongs committed by the Canadian government against Japanese Canadians. In recent months we'd been negotiating with Gerry Weiner, the Minister of State for Multiculturalism and Citizenship – the latest in a long series of government representatives. But the talks had become stalled. On August 10, 1988, help came from an unlikely source. American President Ronald Reagan signed the Civil Liberties Act, compensating Japanese Americans for their wartime loss of freedom. The U.S. action clearly placed more pressure on the Mulroney administration to settle one of its worst nagging headaches.

Unlike other politicians we'd dealt with, Weiner had been prepared to listen. Fiftyish, tall, and long-faced, Weiner brought a somewhat rumpled-looking presence to our meetings. He had invariably been sympathetic and genial in our committee's dealings with him. His stern features could change dramatically whenever the opportunity for a joke came up. A former small-town pharmacist turned mayor, and a self-proclaimed habitué of Montreal's St. Urbain Street, Weiner seemed a natural politician, full of Yiddish humour and charm. Encouraged by Mulroney to strike a deal with the NAJC, he had acted the part of fence-mender, anxious to keep all sides talking.

On August 24, in the Ritz-Carlton's Chambre de Conseil, we met the other governmental staffers: Rick Clippendale, adviser to the minister; Dennison Moore, Weiner's Chief of Staff; Anne Scotton, a Multiculturalism officer; and Alain Bisson, a lawyer from the Department of Justice. Surprisingly, Weiner also introduced us to a more senior cabinet colleague: Lucien Bouchard, the Secretary of State and one of Mulroney's closest friends – a clear sign that finally the government was taking our talks seriously. Bouchard had entered federal politics after a thirty-year association with Mulroney, and almost immediately he had become the prime minister's Quebec lieutenant. In May 1990 – by then the environment minister – he would desert the prime minister over the proposed Meech Lake accord, quitting the cabinet and by all reports leaving a devastated Mulroney.

But that was in the future. At the beginning of our final negotiation sessions in August 1988, Weiner leaned over and whispered – loud enough for all of us to hear – that Bouchard was one of the very few in Parliament who could pick up the phone and call Mulroney and say, "Brian, this is Lucien," and immediately get to talk to the P.M. Bouchard moved quickly to the business at hand. He said he had been given the authority to speak for the prime minister and that over the next few days we'd be having important discussions that could settle our claim for compensation once and for all. We perked up our ears and anxiously awaited the minister's pronouncement. For the first time in the long years of determined pressure it felt like we were on the verge of reaching an accord.

But there was still serious negotiating to do. Bouchard informed us that the NAJC's demand for individual compensation was "too high." He said the government wanted a "Canadian solution," which meant providing "a lower amount to individuals, but an immediate payout." This was an important concession: previous talks had stalled over the government's opposition to individual compensation. When we asked Bouchard what amount he had in mind, he said $15,000 a survivor, with all monies to be dispensed within two years from the date of signing. Amazingly, the government had moved from a previous "high" offer of a $12 million total payout to an offer that would in the end amount to some $400 million.

After this pronouncement, Bouchard kept his cards close to his chest – perhaps a result of his background as a diplomat. He said little else and soon withdrew, promising we could get in touch with him at any time during the negotiations if we needed to. The rest of us got down to work, carefully going over the NAJC's redress proposal point by point – stopping now and then to wolf down enormous corned beef sandwiches that Gerry Weiner ordered in from his favourite Montreal deli. We kept telling Weiner that if he kept plying us with such good food, we would never end the meetings. Three days later, after some seventeen hours of negotiations, we had hashed out a deal.

Among other things the settlement contained the following provisions: a government acknowledgement of the injustice done to Japanese Canadians during the Second World War; a $21,000 payment to each survivor; $12 million to the Japanese Canadian community, to be administered by the NAJC, for educational, social, and cultural activities and programs; and $24 million for a jointly funded Canadian Race Relations Foundation to foster racial harmony and help fight racism. We hoped that the terms of our settlement would help to ensure that other groups in Canada would not have to relive our history.

When the draft agreement was signed on August 27, Weiner warned us not to get our hopes up too high, because the "whole thing could be called off." There was a possibility that the deal might not go through. As if taking their cue from the minister, the other government negotiators at the table also drummed into us the warning that a leak from either their camp or ours could endanger the whole settlement. The bureaucrats wanted to make sure that as few government employees as possible were informed of the agreement. It was common knowledge that there was opposition to the idea of redress, particularly among war veterans. Weiner warned us that the government was concerned "about a back-lash."

From our side, we knew that given our community's close-knit nature and the joy that news of the deal would bring, our negotiating team would simply have to keep its collective mouth shut. Otherwise the secret would spread along the country's phone lines in a matter of a few hours – even if whispered, of course, in the strictest of confidence. During the following weeks our anxieties only increased as no word of the agreement came through. Instead the press seemed content with its endless speculation on when the prime minister would call the fall 1988 election. In the background, the clock was ticking loudly; this session of Parliament was almost over. Already, time constraints had eliminated the possibility of a Japanese Canadian redress bill. New legislation required three readings in the House of Commons as well as passage through the Senate, so it seemed the democratic trimmings were becoming annoyingly time-consuming.

Life was not unfolding as it should. Ideally, from my perspective, ratification of our settlement would have included an all-party resolution acknowledging government wrongdoing– followed by a Japanese Canadian redress act that would stand as the law of the land. It may be my legalistic background, but I believe that laws can safeguard us from our politicians. As the days passed by, the options seemed to narrow. The government officials explained that once an election was called, all the M.P.s would head home to begin campaigning, and that life on the hill would grind to a halt. We would have to be satisfied with a cabinet decision, spelled out as an Order-in-Council. In the middle of September a government official confirmed that there would be no all-party resolution because Mulroney didn't want to run the risk of having to renegotiate the agreement with the other parties. Later we were also told that he had been afraid of the opposition he would face within his own party – indeed, within his cabinet.

Meanwhile, for me the elusive prime minister began to take on mythical proportions. He would appear in my dreams, one time sitting alone in the corner booth of a neighbourhood Hungarian greasy spoon. He was finishing a plate of blintzes and sour cream. Another time he was talking at night in a telephone booth under my second-floor window. Invariably he'd be dressed to kill, no five o'clock shadow, all hairs in place. He was always surrounded by a mob of giants. I would try to fight my way through his cortège to get to the prime minister's table or catch him before he hung up the phone, only to wake up breathless just as he slipped into a waiting limousine.

In my waking hours I mentally rehearsed the alternate pleas that I would have made if only I could talk to him: for the Irishman, a heart-rending story; for the lawyer, a glint of steel perhaps. I pondered the logistical problem that even if I did catch up, given our height difference (I'm five feet tall) I would have had to whisper my message into his chest and not in his ear. I wouldn't have a box to stand on like they do in the Hollywood movies. In my mind I began planning agit prop theatre that involved trailing after Mulroney during the fall election campaign. I envisaged a saffron-robed monk carrying only a bedroll and ringing a small Buddhist gong, following the prime minister's caravan across the country. The smell of the burning incense would linger, coating the clothes of the prime minister's entourage and unforgettably stinging their nostrils. The monk would be accompanied by three Japanese Canadian women representing our different generations in this country: an *issei* (first generation), a *nisei* (second generation), and a *sansei* (third generation). All dressed in black, the women would sit at the back of Mulroney's press conferences casting spells and muttering curses like Macbeth's witches. Or, like "Shy Monkey," a mythical Japanese heroine who had devised ingenious methods of eradicating her rivals, the crones would stick thin-skinned bamboo toothpicks into their gums and from blackened mouths they would invoke plagues upon the prime minister.

Needless to say, these scenarios remained figments of my imagination.

By the second half of September our group had an inkling that something was in the wind. The Prime Minister's Office had been floating trial balloons in the media to gauge both the level of support and the amount of flack he would receive should he publicly ratify the agreement. On September 20 and 21, NAJC President Art Miki started getting phone calls from reporters about a possible settlement. Miki was walking on eggs. At first he feared a leak from our side, but he was reassured to learn that the callers had got the information from the PMO itself. Across the country the NAJC negotiators all breathed a collective sigh of relief. We had heard that this was the way Mulroney operated. His office routinely sent out feelers to test the waters, and if things looked safe he would proceed. Nonetheless, Miki buttoned his lips and revealed only that the NAJC was having continuing discussions with the government and that things were looking up.

A few days later we were again surprised when the press published new reports of a settlement. The prime minister had made his move. Having been reassured that the war veterans organizations would not openly oppose the redress agreement and that minority organizations in Canada would applaud him, Mulroney had apparently decided to announce this significant civil rights agreement on the eve of calling his second election.

Flying to Ottawa on September 21 with the other Toronto committee member, Roger Obata, I felt immensely relieved. Finally I could rid myself of this secret that like a tourniquet had been slowly tightening around my chest.

The whole experience of officially prescribed secrecy had made me feel like Mosaku, the apprentice woodcutter in an old Japanese fable about Yuki-Onna, the snow woman. According to the legend, on a winter's evening an old master woodcutter and his apprentice, Mosaku, sought refuge from a blizzard in a tiny, unheated hut. As they slept, a beautiful white snow queen spirit entered the cabin and blew her cold breath on the old master's body, turning it to ice. As the snow queen was stooping over Mosaku's face, about to do the same to him, she was struck by his youthful beauty and decided to let him live. When Mosaku awoke she warned him that if he ever told anyone about what he had seen, she would return to kill him.

A year later Mosaku chanced to meet a beautiful pale-skinned girl with the voice of a songbird. She was named O-Yuki (snow). Recently orphaned, O-Yuki was travelling alone on the road to Yedo to seek assistance from some of her relatives. The young woodcutter, immediately entranced, persuaded the girl to delay her journey and rest a while with his family. Of course the young couple fell deeply in love. They married, prospered, and had numerous beautiful children. But even with the passage of many years, the woodcutter's wife, to the amazement of the other villagers, remained as young and fresh looking as the day she had first come to the hamlet.

One night, the sight of O-Yuki sitting peacefully sewing by the light of a paper lantern reminded Mosaku of that winter's evening long before when he had met another woman as beautiful and fair. He carelessly told O-Yuki the story. As soon as the fateful secret had been recounted, O-Yuki screamed out that she was the snow queen spirit and that only for the love of her children would she again spare the tattletale's life. O-Yuki's voice became like the crying of the wind, and she melted into a bright white mist that spiralled up the smoke-hole of the cottage, gone forever. For his indiscretion Mosaku was never again to know the comfort or company of her love.

Our committee's secret, with the heavy weight of the Canadian government behind it, seemed just as precious as Mosaku's, and the whole thing had made me anxious. Spontaneously I had nonetheless confided the news of our settlement to my husband. Then I chanced to ask Roger Obata how his wife Mary had reacted to our August agreement. To my surprise, Roger, a seventy-five-year-old nisei, a Canadian war veteran, and a successful engineer-businessman, said he had not told his wife about the deal, because of the oath of secrecy. I immediately felt guilty and began to wonder what Mosaku-like punishment was in store for me. Later I discovered that I wasn't alone: all of the other sansei or third generation members of the negotiating team had also confided this secret to their spouses, despite the security warnings.

Roger's taciturnity was surely another manifestation of nisei self-control and an indication of our generational differences. It was as though with each decade spent away from that chain of volcanic islands in the Pacific Ocean we were losing our ancestors' iron-like Japanese core. Irritatingly, Roger is also astonishingly energetic. After our NAJC Council meetings, which would often wind up in the early morning hours, Roger and the other nisei men, many over sixty, would head out to an all-night Chinese restaurant for a bowl of *soba* – buckwheat noodles in chicken broth. Coming back in time to catch a few hours of sleep before the sessions reconvened in the morning, their stamina easily surpassed the younger sansei.

Undoubtedly that strengthened the nisei's cultural prejudices against the sansei, whom they regarded to be as feckless as their children. Their agism was something fierce, as equally a virulent strain as their sexism. The NAJC Council, ninety per cent male with an average age in the early sixties, mirrored our community's traditionalism. Roger used to say that he and Harold Hirose, a charming, respected seventy-six-year-old nisei, had both remained on as NAJC vice-president and treasurer respectively because Sisco, the seventy-seven-year-old mother of President Art Miki, had told them that the "kids," namely her fifty-five-year-old son Art – now a grandfather himself– "needed their guidance." Occasionally, when irritated by this seemingly impenetrable wall of tradition, I would let slip, "Even the Chinese Canadian National Council, for God's sake, has had a woman president who was in her thirties." Undoubtedly there would have been gasps as grey heads fainted dead away at even the thought of such a development.

When we got to Ottawa on September 21, Roger Obata and I found ourselves put up at a charming downtown bed and breakfast house. We soon discovered that the other members of the NAJC team were scattered around the city in similarly out of the way places. The Secretary of State staff said these arrangements were necessary because all the hotel rooms in Ottawa were solidly booked and they couldn't manage to get us all rooms together. We accepted this explanation but soon came up with a theory of our own: the department wanted to maintain absolute control over this important media event. The bureaucrats were afraid that if the Ottawa press saw us all troop into the Chateau Laurier, the cat would have been let out of the bag. They reasoned that if we were separately tucked away in various spots that news hounds were unlikely to sniff out, a properly orchestrated story would only break out when the prime minister wanted it to: that is, when he began his speech the next day at eleven o'clock in the House of Commons.

After breakfast on September 22, Roger and I headed off across the river to Hull for a rushed morning meeting with the Secretary of State staff, followed by a second briefing in Gerry Weiner's office back on Parliament Hill. Then uniformed guards led the NAJC negotiators through the back corridors of the Parliament building to the Visitors Gallery of the House of Commons. As we filed into seats high above the opposition benches, Prime Minister Mulroney briefly glanced up at us – looking every bit as good as he had in my dreams. I saw that seniors from the Ottawa Japanese Canadian community were seated on the other side of the House. Mulroney's press aides had let slip that they wanted lots of grey-haired Japanese Canadians present for the "photo opportunities."

Mulroney began his prepared speech: "Nearly half a century ago, in the crisis of wartime, the Government of Canada wrongfully incarcerated, seized the property, and disenfranchised thousands of citizens of Japanese ancestry. We cannot change the past. But we must, as a nation, have the courage to face up to these historical facts." Mulroney said that "words and laws" weren't enough and that his colleague Gerry Weiner would soon be announcing the full details of the settlement. He added, "No amount of money can right the wrong, undo the harm, and heal the wounds. But it is symbolic of our determination to address this issue, not only in the moral sense, but also in a tangible way." He paused and looked up at us again, as he acknowledged the years of determined pressure that had brought the government to the settlement table. Tears were brimming in my eyes as I proudly witnessed the most gratifying event in our community's history.

The irony in the situation escaped me at the time. Later we found out that when the prime minister made his announcement only four members of the government – Mulroney himself, Weiner, Bouchard, and Donald Mazankowski – knew the exact terms of the agreement. Even with the pivotal retirement in July 1988 of Veteran Affairs minister George Hees, a strong opponent of redress, it seems that Mulroney, knowing the opposition that he would face in cabinet, had made the decision virtually alone.

Although the precedent established by the settlement strengthened the democratic rights of all Canadians, the manner in which it was arrived at was disturbing. The Japanese Canadian community had lost its democratic rights in the 1940s through the cloak and dagger machinations of the Mackenzie King government. Now an "enlightened monarch," acting autocratically without the full knowledge of Parliament, had corrected those wrongs. In both instances – the 1942 decision to intern the "enemy aliens" and the 1988 gesture to compensate the surviving victims – Canada, marionette-like, had followed the American lead. Less than two weeks after President Reagan had signed the Civil Rights Act, authorizing a $1.25 billion payment to American Japanese, the NAJC's negotiators were hammering out the agreement in Montreal.

After his speech Mulroney sat down to thunderous applause and a standing ovation. Ed Broadbent, leader of the New Democratic Party, seemed close to tears as he walked across the floor to congratulate the prime minister on the government's actions. Later Broadbent spoke of his party's historical support for the Japanese Canadian community. Broadbent's first wife, a Japanese Canadian, had spent the war years at the same relocation camp as my own family. Sergio Marchi, the Liberal Party's multiculturalism critic, also congratulated the prime minister, Art Miki, and the NAJC for closing "the chapter of what was a very sad and sensitive memory in our history." Marchi was standing in for Liberal leader John Turner, who was already on the campaign trail in British Columbia. Although Marchi promised that Turner would make a statement of support later in the day, as far as I know Turner never did. This was not so surprising: the Liberal leader had always been, at best, lukewarm in his support for the NAJC redress package.

The parliamentary process was all over in what seemed like a matter of minutes. While most of the opposition members stood to applaud, I noticed pockets of Tories still rooted in their seats, arms folded firmly across their chests: a tangible sign of their firm opposition to redress. A few days after the announcement I read the angry criticism by one Tory backbencher, Ron Stewart of Barrie, Ontario, as reported in *The Toronto Star*. Stewart said that the agreement was "just a windfall profit" for the Japanese Canadians. "I can't be very sympathetic. I don't know what was going through the Prime Minister's mind." About a dozen Conservative M.P.s – many of them war veterans – were reported to have "serious reservations about the compensation package."[1]

The attitudes of these men reminded me of the historic "Conference on Japanese Problems" held in Ottawa on January 8-9, 1942 and chaired by the B.C. M.P. Ian Mackenzie, an acknowledged racist and the federal Minister of Pensions. Soon afterwards, on February 24, 1942, the B.C. politicians were successful in convincing cabinet to uproot the entire

Japanese Canadian community. According to Escott Reid, a special assistant in the Department of External Affairs at the time, "They spoke of the Japanese Canadians in the way that the Nazis would have spoken about Jewish Germans. When they spoke, I felt in that committee room the physical presence of evil." The comment was echoed by General Maurice Pope, who said, "I came away from that meeting feeling dirty all over."[2] Sitting in the House of Commons, forty-six years later, I wondered if opinions in the Tory caucus had changed much since the days of Ian Mackenzie. Privately I thanked Brian Mulroney for "honouring his word" to us.

Seconds after the speeches were over, the House moved onto other business. I was surprised. I don't know what I expected, but I had thought that after we had spent years of our lives to get those premium seats in the House of Commons, somehow the victorious moment would have lasted more than a few minutes and taken up more than several lines on the government's order paper. It was all so cut and dried. I found myself wanting more than speeches: perhaps a public bloodletting. Minimally Ian Mackenzie brought back and made to eat his tartan; for William Lyon Mackenzie King, a steady diet of tap water and stacks of the dry War Measures Act Order-in-Council papers.

As if reading my mind, guards quickly ushered us out and government aides herded us through a maze of drafty, cold marble corridors into the stately Confederation Room, which was filled with dozens of photographers and reporters. At the front of the room, cordoned off from the press, was a long table covered with piles of gold, red, and blue state documents, some in English and some in French. Those of us on the negotiating team, along with Lucien Bouchard and Gerry Weiner, were led to seats directly behind where Art Miki and the prime minister were to sit, all of us facing the hot flood-lit cameras. Minutes later there was a round of applause when the two men entered the room and shook hands. As the cameras clicked and rolled Mulroney and Miki signed the official documents that meant so much in so many ways to our Japanese Canadian community. Incredibly, with a simple stroke of the pen, the prime minister had imperiously returned honour and dignity to an entire community.

Afterwards Mulroney got up and came and shook hands with each one of us – I finally got to meet the man in my dreams, face to face, to see him at close range. I'd have something to tell my mother, who was always asking me, "What's he like?" Mostly I remember noticing his pale, beautiful, long curly eyelashes. He had nothing in particular to say except, "Congratulations on a job well done." Given the intensity of the moment, I'm not sure how coherent any of us would have been if he had tried to engage us in more than small talk.

Then, as quickly as he had come, he left. The camera lights went off, the air chilled instantly, and the room slowly cleared as the reporters gathered up their bags and equipment – some of them would be going to cover the press conference on the settlement that was scheduled to start soon just across the street. Our own group also left the Parliament buildings, crossed Wellington Street, and made its way to the National Press Building. A seated guard half-heartedly tried to keep us out by telling us that only members of the Press Gallery were being allowed in. But there was no way that, having come so far, we were going to miss this next event. We filed in and grabbed the few empty chairs left near the back of the crowded room in time to hear Gerry Weiner, seated at a table at the front, read out the terms of the agreement. Then Weiner and Art Miki responded to questions from the reporters.

The mood was friendly. Still, the previous four years had been a trial by ordeal for Art Miki, who had earned his stripes after years of being our public spokesman. His square face with the childhood scar jaggedly running across the left cheek and his school principal's penchant for lengthy, earnest speeches may not have been the first choice of a movie casting director. He lacked the flamboyance of scientist-journalist David Suzuki or the eloquence of the author of *Obasan*, Joy Kogawa, but in so many ways he exemplified us, the everyday Japanese Canadian: honest, stubborn, a consensus builder, a devoted family person, a community supporter. Art's sheer doggedness had maintained us through those years and the community will be forever in his debt. Although at times we may have wished for a more charismatic public persona, perhaps in the end it was his straightforward nature that helped make the media and the Canadian people sympathetic.

Looking down on the country's press, who were sandwiched between Miki, Weiner, and the spectator gallery, I was struck by their youth and energy. Drawn to the hot lights, plugged into thick electric sockets, they were gathered together in a shimmering swarm. This group of reporters, the country's fifth estate, seemed almost oblivious to the power they wielded. Daily it was their words and images that shaped our sense of the world. Over the years, they had impressed me with their profound sense of justice – and also with their ignorance of the issue, and their almost adolescent laziness. They knew nothing of our culture and history, and they were willing to rely on hackneyed stereotypes. In their training they been taught that balanced impartial reporting meant describing at least two of the many sides of every story. But we had relied on their intelligence and fairness. We had met with many of them to explain our struggle and to try to influence their coverage. Without exception they were convinced by indisputable documentation and hard facts. In the end they did turn out to be on our side, which gives me hope for our country. Privately, after the press conference was over, several reporters came over to me with congratulations. Some of them had mistaken me for the author Joy Kogawa. One of them told me that the National Press Gallery had been profoundly affected by only two stories: the free vote against the reinstatement of the death penalty, and the government's decision "to do the right thing" on Japanese Canadian redress.

After the room had emptied, we were guided back across the street to the Confederation Room for a reception. Politicians and the press, various community leaders, and local Ottawa Japanese Canadians were present and nibbling. As I circulated about the room, chatting with well-wishers and long-time supporters, I felt pleasantly unconnected to reality – by then the day had taken on its own dream-like quality. It seemed as though we were actors playing out the closing scene of an epic drama that fortunately had a happy ending.

Afterwards, we went up to Weiner's office where his aide, Dennison Moore, broke open two bottles of champagne. Heartily we drank toasts to each other's health, then we were crowded into several cars and rushed to the Ottawa airport. Our day of celebration wasn't over yet: the Minister's office had organized a large reception and celebration back in Toronto. We were scheduled to get there minutes before the event was to begin.

The Sutton Place Hotel's banquet-hall was packed with Metro Toronto's "multicultural" establishment, who were being wooed for the upcoming fall election. I avoided the jaundiced regulars, who were whispering cynically about the implications of the redress settlement. Wanting to savour our success and enjoy our victory, I found myself sticking to my own. For once in our one-hundred-and-ten-year history in this country, Japanese Canadians had reason to be proud and to celebrate. During the next few hours I must have embraced at least half of the several hundred Japanese Canadian supporters in the room. I gladly welcomed congratulations from some of our "foes" in the Japanese Canadian community – those people who had opposed the NAJC's leadership because they, unlike the NAJC, had been willing to accept whatever small crumbs the government was willing to offer.

By seven o'clock the crowd was beginning to thin out as the celebrants began to make their way home in the late rush-hour traffic. Although there was a fine drizzle, the evening was still warm as we crowded into cars and cabs for a celebratory dinner. According to ritual, some of us headed straight for a Chinese restaurant. We had ended countless late-night meetings with the friendly communal sharing of honey garlic ribs and steamed fresh pickerel in black bean sauce, while squeezed tightly around large formica tables. Surrounded by friends and co-workers, I could feel the day's tension and stress begin to dissipate into the steam above our endless cups of green tea.

Immediately following Toronto's multicultural event, Gerry Weiner had flown straight to Vancouver. By contrast, Vancouver's announcement was a Japanese Canadian affair. That evening, the entire community turned out to meet the minister at the Japanese language school in old Japantown. Afterwards Weiner and a large mob invaded a Japanese restaurant on Powell Street whose owner Aki, a longtime redress supporter, had closed his restaurant to other customers, and cooked up a storm. Consuming large quantities of sushi, grilled chicken, and beer, the party lasted until the early morning rays of the sun began to pierce through the *shoji* screens.

That evening and on the following day, the settlement dominated the front pages of the daily newspapers and the news broadcasts. Across the country, in throng-filled halls and around kitchen tables, Japanese Canadians celebrated the return of their dignity. The community had regained its honour at last. Going home that night in the quiet darkness of the car, with three of us pressed together in the back seat, I thought of my mother, brother, and sister, all in Hamilton. They would have heard the news, and I wished I was there with them. It was a time to be near those we loved – the people who had gone through the painful years and who daily still bore the scars.

McGillivray Falls. B.C. April. 4ᵗʰ 1943.

Omatsu family in group photo with members of the McGillivray Falls, B.C. self-supporting community, 1943.

2 | On Being An Alien

As final resting place,
Canada is chosen.
On citizenship paper,
Signing
Hand trembles.

– Tanka by Takeo Ujo Nakano commemorating his
receipt of Canadian citizenship. Translation by
Leatrice Nakano Willson

I AM A CANADIAN by nationality and citizenship and a Japanese by
ancestry. Almost one hundred years ago my ancestors set off for a place
they called "Amerika," leaving forever Nippon, the land of the Rising
Sun. The Chinese called the archipelago Jih-pen, the sunrise islands.
Europeans hearing this Chinese appellation converted it to Japan and its
inhabitants to the Japanese.[1] Privately we call ourselves Nihon-jin
(Nihon-Japan, jin-people).

In all of China, I am told, there are only four hundred and seventy sur-
names. In Japan there are countless thousands, although until the mid-
nineteenth century only noble and samurai families were given those
names. My family name, Omatsu, is a relatively recent acquisition. It
means pine tree. It wasn't until 1990, when I visited my father's ancestoral
home in Shiga-ken outside of Kyoto, that I understood how we came
upon that designation.

I am writing this book by the Gregorian calendar in the year 1991, by

Japanese computation in the third year of the Heisei reign (eternal peace). Akihito, the present emperor, is the eldest son of Hirohito and the one hundred and twenty-fifth to sit on the Chrysanthemum throne, the world's longest imperial dynasty. Akihito, it is said, can trace his lineage back to Jimmu, the first emperor who founded the kingdom in 660 B.C. and who, according to legend, was a descendant of Amaterasu, the Goddess of the Sun. By Japanese reckoning I am a sansei, three generations away from the land where my family has lived since time immemorial. Canadians, discounting my grandparents, consider me a second-generation Canadian.

I see the world as if through bifocals, with my Japanese lenses overlaid by my Canadian ones – or is it the other way around? On occasion this mixed vision makes me feel puzzled and disoriented, as bifocals sometimes do. Generally I think it makes my life dizzyingly rich and varied. I know that my ancestral past has an increasingly strong hold on the person I am becoming, yet I no longer share the religion, language, and culture of my grandparents. I mourn the loss of the daily-weakening ties that bind me to the land of the rising sun. I am not alone. My cultural story, with its exhilarating infusion of the new and the confusing loss of the past, is the reality of all immigrants, and especially of those of us from non-European cultures.

When my father died in 1981 at the age of eighty, we were virtual strangers. Our five-decade gap in ages was widened by a cultural century's divide. With barely a language in common to bridge Japan's Meiji era (1868-1912) and the twentieth century, we existed in the same house as if in two separate time capsules. Now, a decade later, I am just beginning to know and like the man. Shortly after his death I returned to his small sunlit bedroom in our family house in Hamilton, Ontario, to go through his personal effects. As usual, as if he was expected to return at any moment, his bed was made and his clothes were carefully hung in the closet. His bookcase shelves were neatly organized, although they were now caught in a losing battle with my mother, who had almost completely taken over the shelves with her stacks of sweet-smelling linens. Father's desk was cleared except for some old newspapers and magazines, and his chest of drawers was covered with religious artifacts and photos of deceased family members, most of whom I had never met. Tucked under the bed were his worn felt slippers; my mother had taken his newer leather ones to the hospital.

To me his room, like the man himself, was ordinary and yet alien. On one wall hung a Japanese wood-block scroll depicting a crane at the base of a mountain shrouded in mist, a stylized scene set thousands of miles away. His magazines and newspapers were written in what were to me indecipherable Japanese characters. He had arranged a few yellowing photos of my unknown relatives on a small Buddhist altar around which lingered, as usual, the faint scent of recently burnt incense.

In preparation for his death, my father, always the accountant, had organized his papers and balanced his finances. All his worldly and prized possessions fit into one drawer. Going through his wallet, I found his plastic Canadian citizenship card, his Hamilton senior citizens transit card, and – tucked away in a back compartment and neatly folded – his worn World War II government-issued "enemy alien" identification card, complete with his photo and thumb print. During the war and for a time after, all Japanese Canadians were legally required to carry these numbered identification cards. They had to produce them upon request by police and government officials.

Sitting on his bed, with his lifetime spread out around me, I felt anger and sadness upon seeing that tattered document– anger at the government that had "tattooed" my father and sadness for the man who had always lived in fear. It wasn't until years later that I would understand why.

At many of the hundreds of redress meetings I have spoken at, helped organized, or attended over many years, I am regularly asked if I am related to such and such a person. Often, because the Japanese Canadian community is small and closely knit, it turns out that I am. A smile will cross the face of the questioner, and on occasion I'll be told a previously unknown story about my father or my family. At one of those events I learned that my father had once been incarcerated for improper identification. During and after the war, Japanese Canadians were held in detention camps, denied freedom of movement, and made subject to a dawn to dusk curfew. My father had applied to the RCMP for a permit to travel to another town to look for work. The officer, unfamiliar with Japanese names, had misspelt his name and instead of writing "Omatsu" had written something approximating it. Later on, when officials asked my father to show his identification papers and found the wrong name, my father was thrown into jail, without a trial, for "travelling without authority."

My father, apparently shamed by this episode, went to his grave with the secret. Perhaps the incident explains why in spite of his warning to me that no one would go to a woman attorney, he nonetheless supported my ambition to become a criminal defence lawyer in the mid-1970s, at a time when you could count on two hands the number of female members of the criminal bar in the whole country.

Secrets: dear father, if only you hadn't weighed yourself down with so many secrets. But how could you have kept from me your darkest secret? Never once did we speak of your wartime experiences. Unbelievably, you let me learn about the most central event in your life from my grade twelve history textbook, which reduced your incarceration, property confiscation, and degradation to four lines. Somehow I memorized those four lines for my history examination without connecting them to you or to me. But the fault is not all yours. Years later, when an occasion arose again, I kept my own silence.

In 1980, when you were nearing eighty years of age and you knew that your travelling days were almost over, you decided to take a last trip back to Vancouver to remember what were, in retrospect, the best years of your life. You planned this journey with exactitude. A few times before, for the occasional family funeral or reunion in British Columbia, you had flown directly to the west coast. This time however, you and my mother wanted to relive your first train ride over the Rocky Mountains, to recreate what must have been an extremely stress-filled and memory-laden period. When you returned home from your visit out west, you told me about spending an afternoon in downtown Vancouver, seeking out the corner where your restaurant had once been. Forty years later you could still drink tea in the coffee shop of your old competitor, amazingly still in business. Your own restaurant had long since changed hands and was now a shiny new bank branch-office.

The year before you died, Denny Boyd, a *Vancouver Sun* columnist, had "a half-buried memory of a Japanese-run place at Broadway and Granville, where the Royal Bank is, where, prior to the 1941 panic, you could get a cheeseburger and a milkshake for two bits." You were pleased and proud to be included in a column in which Boyd paid tribute to "a few restaurants or chains through the decades and the generations; that were always distinctively Vancouver, that created almost an emotional loyalty among their patrons."[2] I still have the yellowing newspaper clipping and a copy of a letter that I sent Boyd on your behalf, thanking him for remembering and cheering up an old man.

Now, every time I am in Vancouver and I pass your corner I am filled with an anger so palpable that my mouth starts tasting of dry sawdust. I knew that you missed British Columbia with the longing of a lost love. After all, how could you forget the rain-drenched lushness and the staggering beauty of the mountains backdropping the Pacific Ocean? Still, I could understand why you never returned there. Just turning a corner would have unleashed memories that would have eventually consumed you. When I go by the area where you grew up in Kitsilano, I resist an urge to find your family's house and boldly knock on the front door. Perhaps in an attic or deep in a basement someplace I would find a memento that would tie me to you. But instead I drive through the area, only slowing down momentarily to visually memorize your neighbourhood. When I pass elderly *hakujin* (whites), I can't help wondering if any of them had cheered when the "Japs" were forced to leave town. Did any of your faithful customers in Vancouver protest or even say they were sorry when they saw a "for sale" sign go up in your shop window?

Your goal was to forget, to numb the mind, to blot out the years. We all knew people in the community who had been unable to contain the memories. They were the ones whispered about, who went mad or died by their own hand. But by the spring of 1980 you were unafraid of death and finally free to relive your past. On that retrospective trip, did your memories flood back to the hot day in June 1948 when you had boarded a CPR train in Revelstoke, British Columbia, bound for Ontario? Perhaps it was not just anxiety you felt in the pit of your stomach but also hope. Perhaps you felt a sense of relief. You were surrounded by your two children, your wife pregnant with me, and the family possessions crammed into a few suitcases and cardboard boxes. Finally you had been let out. Finally, after six years of uncertainty, they were going to let you live a normal life.

Dear father, could you have really been hopeful? In 1948 you were almost fifty, an "enemy alien," homeless, unemployed, with a dependent wife and children. You were virtually penniless because the government had made you spend all of your life's savings to pay for your five years of captivity. Did you know how difficult it would be to start over? Free at last, you must have sighed– free thanks largely to a public outcry that had been organized by civil libertarians, the churches, and the Co-operative Commonwealth Federation (CCF). For years they had all been questioning why Canadians of Japanese ancestry were still being held in detention camps long after the end of the war. The Canadian government had hoped to solve the "Japanese Canadian problem" by carrying out massive deportations to postwar Japan. Despite supportive legal decisions going all the way up to the Privy Council in England that the deportation orders-in-council were legal, a public campaign reduced the number of Japanese Canadians who were finally deported or exiled to about four thousand.

Nonetheless, not all wartime restrictions were lifted. You and all other Canadians of Japanese ancestry were still denied freedom of movement. You were prohibited from returning to the "one-hundred mile zone" along the west coast where most of the community had lived until 1942. Throughout the years of forced relocation and detention you had wondered what had happened to your restaurant and dreamed of suddenly waking up surrounded by the hustle and bustle of customers and the smell of freshly made coffee. In 1948 the federal and B.C. governments did not want homeless, unemployed, and destitute Japanese Canadians returning to their homes, farms, and businesses, which were by then owned by veterans or persons who had benefited from the 1942 government-held fire sales. But in 1980 no one thought to stop a small, white-haired Japanese Canadian from staring wistfully at a dream that had faded with time.

In 1948 the federal government of Prime Minister Mackenzie King had given you two choices: exile/deportation to Japan or relocation east of the Rocky Mountains. You felt as though you had a gun pointed at your head. Although at first the governments of both British Columbia and Alberta refused to accept the bedraggled aliens of a now defeated enemy, in the end, Alberta, desperate for sugar-beet workers, did assume its share. But you, like most of the remaining eighteen thousand, opted for relocation in the east. You chose to resettle in Hamilton partly because my mother, who had been born in the rugged mountains of British Columbia and who loved the snow-capped Rockies, had heard there was a "mountain" there. Did you laugh or cry when you saw the escarpment that is called Hamilton Mountain? Still, rumour had it that it was better in Ontario, that there was less racism there.

In 1980, when you came back from that trip to the coast, your past, which was our shared history, remained unspoken; we still did not speak of the war years. Perhaps neither of us is to blame for not unlocking that painful memory. Your culture, where much is unsaid but understood, directed you to accept the dark past with resignation, to bury shame and dishonour, and to strive to carry on. Yet deep in your heart you never forgot or forgave what they had done. All of this left me feeling like Alice in Wonderland continually stepping in and out of the looking glass. Growing up in the 1950s I always expected to find myself living the idealized WASP existence of the televised families I was seeing every week on *Ozzie and Harriet, Leave It to Beaver,* or *Father Knows Best.* But when I examined my face in the mirror I knew that an alien blood flowed in my veins, just as it had in yours.

Now I understand that you, like all the other Japanese Canadian parents I have spoken with, hoped that by not evoking the past you could somehow shield us, your children, from it. Perhaps you thought that by not sharing your culture and language with us we would not be tarred by it. But despite all your good intentions we remained both cut off from our ancestral past and scarred by our history in this country. In the end you were unable to protect us from that debilitating virus that invaded our homes and our very souls. It filled me with a shame that I could not understand as a child. One evening you came to walk me home from a Brownie meeting. Holding your hand as I excitedly described the secret knots I had just learned, a group of boys yelled at us: "Chink, Chink." I immediately dropped your hand and if I could have I would have crossed the street. We walked home in silence. I still carry with me my childhood feelings of fear and self-hatred. There is no inoculation against this virus.

Oftentimes powerless, I have felt programmed by forces I do not fully comprehend. Honour and duty are like two electrodes that have been implanted in my brain. These electrodes held our redress struggle together. Throughout the years they have given us the strength to continue even on the dark, hopeless days. We, a genetically disappearing people, were obligated to clear our names before we blended into the amorphous Canadian background. We owed this to our ancestors, who in spite of the racism of the time remained in this country. We owe it to our offspring, who will conceivably share with us only a slight slant of the eyelids or a darkened blush of the skin. Or perhaps our alien culture was transmitted in our mother's milk. How else to explain its ability to direct and shape our very emotions?

Several years ago I went to see a Japanese movie, *The Funeral,* directed by one of the country's most celebrated filmmakers, Juzo Itami. I was with Marcia Matsui, a Japanese Canadian lawyer, and two non-Japanese Canadian friends. The plot centres around the funeral of a parent of a present-day middle-class Tokyo family. The bereaved adults have to rent videos to learn how to exhibit the expected protocol and requisite behaviour. Marcia and I were the only Japanese Canadians in a rather artsy cinema crowd.

Soon after the initial dimming of the lights, and until the closing credits, Marcia and I were convulsed in laughter. With tears streaming down our faces, we laughed, leaning against one another for support. Yet all around us the white faces were impenetrable and impassive. At the end of the movie we looked at one another in amazement. How was it that we, third-generation Canadians like so many of the other filmgoers that night, shared a sense of humour that was so foreign? It dawned on us: we really were aliens.

Ken Adachi, a sixty-one year old Japanese Canadian nisei, was a respected newspaper literary editor and a well-known figure in the Canadian arts community. He was also a personage in the Japanese Canadian community because he had written the first history of our lives in this country. In 1989 his regular *Toronto Star* column contained several paragraphs that were copied from *Time* magazine and after the discovery Adachi was forced to resign from his job. He later committed suicide.

I remember thinking, when I heard the news of his death, that Adachi's actions had been directed by that same alien force thousands of miles away: a power so strong that it could indeed control life or death. In his own eyes he had been personally dishonoured; moreover, because of his prestige, he felt the Japanese Canadian community had been disgraced. His suicide was the act of a logical man. Although I wept and mourned, I empathized. White friends implied that Ken Adachi must have been depressed and psychologically unstable. They did not understand.

To belong, to be accepted and respected. No punishment is worse than to be exiled, cut off, and spat upon. In the playground when we were children, whenever our mothers wanted to gather us up they would run ahead. Fearful of being left behind, we would quickly follow them. The *hakujin*, or white, mothers would scurry around the yard collecting their brood, who would try to escape from being rounded up. When we misbehaved we would not be sent off to our rooms like our schoolmates. No, we would be put out of the house. Out on the front porch we could see the yellow light streaming through the windows and hear the laughter and muffled conversation inside. Eventually shamed and contrite, we would be invited back into the warmth that is family.

Yet when I visited Japan in the early 1970s I felt very Canadian. I found their male chauvinism and rigid behavioural social codes oppressive and restricting. At the same time, in Japan I delighted in my ability to disappear in a crowd, to look like everyone else and to not stick out. Once, when I was arranging by telephone to meet a stranger at a Kyoto metro station, I described myself as a Japanese Canadian woman. At home that would have been all the identification I needed. In Japan my caller, puzzled, said, "But what will you be wearing?" Still I knew I did not belong in Japan.

But growing up in Hamilton during the 1950s and 1960s, I didn't need my reflection in the mirror to tell me that I was different. At times I felt that I was a "normal" person being held captive and raised in a family of "weirdos." How else to explain the fact that my mother always had us bathe *before* we got into the tub, or that my father burned incense and chanted in front of an altar filled with photos of dead relatives? Or that once a year we would make a trek to the grave of my dear baby brother and then join in a community celebration for all our forefathers?

In that respect, going to Japan was an eye-opener. There I found that everyone washed before entering the bath tub. Respect for your ancestors, inaccurately termed ancestor "worship" in Canada, is as Japanese as Mount Fuji. The *O-bon* ceremony to honour deceased relatives, to wish joy for their souls and to remember them, is a national celebration. In Canada there have been days when I imagined myself aboard the *Starship Enterprise* in the television series *Star Trek*. I can see the consternation on the face of first officer Scottie when he has to respond to my order to return me "home." To which country does he "beam" me up?

If perchance, Father, I were to land in our old backyard garden in Hamilton, I would still be confused. For you had tried to create a private oasis that shut out the ugliness of that working-class steel city. You built a fortress-like, six-foot-high, sweet-smelling cedar fence, capped with a wooden peaked roof. This marked the interior walls of a foreign timeless world of stone pagodas and sculptured evergreens, quiet except for the soothing sound of a waterfall. In good weather, lost in thought after work, you would sit in an easy chair until the darkness or the cold would draw you indoors.

Yet our one hundred years in this country have transformed us. We are Canadians in fact, if not by choice. The collective memory that we share with the country of our ancestors dims with each passing year. Heartlessly Canada has jealously demanded that we renounce everything that we hold dear. Still we all have our secret rebellious acts. Clandestinely we hoard our small supplies of Japanese seeds that relatives carefully dispense by the teaspoon-full. Our gardens brim with sweet ladybug-red Japanese tomatoes, long burpless bottle-green cucumbers, and banana-shaped purple eggplants. Only an observant gardener who chances to look over the fence will detect the differences: thinner skins, less seeds, more flavour. Such harmlessness is permitted. In Toronto I notice the small backyard gardens of my Italian, Portuguese, and Chinese neighbours, lush from their own stowaway seeds. Conspiratorially we nod over the back fence.

Father, the only past that you were willing to share with me had an otherworldly aspect to it. Like the crane pictured on the scroll on your bedroom wall, it was shrouded in mist. It was foreign and ancient. At times you would cast your mind back to your early childhood, to a village outside of Kyoto where your family had lived for centuries. You described a garden tranquil with the ever-present sound of flowing water and fragrant from the orange and persimmon blossoms. Your reminiscences of your adolescence in pre-World War I Vancouver seemed almost Dickensian. Your descriptions of horse-drawn carts stuck in muddy ruts and streets illuminated by gas-fed street lamps clearly defined two worlds. The privileged world was white Anglo-Saxon Protestant, the other one was peopled by dark-skinned foreigners. You spoke matter of factly about the publicly posted pay scales: Whites, fifty cents an hour; Asians, twenty-five cents an hour. You had no rancour in your voice, no hatred because of the injustice, yet I remember being filled with anger as I asked, "For exactly the same work as a white man you were paid half?"

You described how as a young delivery boy you got to see the houses on the hill. Sometimes on a cold or wet night in the Shaughnessy area you would be invited into one of the homes while the family searched for the correct change to pay for their prescriptions. You caught fleeting glimpses of crackling fireplaces, shimmering cut-glass chandeliers, and luxurious Persian rugs covering shiny wooden floors.

Ever since those days you had harboured the ambition of living in Shaughnessy in one of those houses. It didn't seem to matter that "Orientals" were explictly prohibited from living there; indeed, laws excluded Japanese Canadians from the best jobs, limiting them to the most menial employment. Nonetheless before the wartime internment your dream actually seemed within your grasp. You had specifically chosen a restaurant location outside of the Japantown ghetto, bordering on Shaughnessy, and the place was doing well. Thanks to a go-between you had married a pretty farm girl. You were able to support your elderly parents, your two children, various relatives, and employees.

Suddenly your face would freeze and the conversation would end. It's as if the clock stopped in January 1942. At the lull I would turn to my mother, who would enthrall me with stories about growing up on a fifteen-acre farm in the Fraser Valley. The oldest child of non-English-speaking Japanese immigrants, she still recalls her first day in a two-room school house. Not speaking a word of English, a tiny frightened girl of six, she had entered with trepidation the largest room she had ever seen. Unlike her white classmates she was made to sit alone on a bench at the front. She didn't know why the teacher was punishing her. The other pupils laughed at her non-existent English and made fun of her rice-ball lunches. She didn't want to return to school, but her father made her go. After six months her English comprehension was good enough so that she could understand the rudiments. Eventually she was given her own desk with the others, and she began to learn. She would return home and proudly read to her parents and younger siblings from a book of fairy tales. She would ask her parents and the other family members whether or not the *hakujin* thought the fairy tales were real. No one was ever sure.

In the end my mother loved school and was a good student. But each fall she would never know whether she would be able to return because of the expense. Somehow her father always managed to scrounge enough money together for her to continue, but as the Depression wore on it became increasingly more difficult. Around the time of her final year of high school her father bought some beehives and said the honey would pay for her high-school graduation. Sales went well until one day provincial officials came to the farm waving papers in their faces. The officials seized all the beehives and equipment and burned them to ashes. Unable to stop them, my grandfather and my mother in tears stood helplessly by. Later they found out that an anglo farm couple down the road, threatened by the competition, had complained to the government that the Japanese were breeding diseased bees that would eventually contaminate the honey of the Fraser Valley. My mother never did finish her last year of high school, but she instilled in me the desire to learn and in fact I was almost thirty before I left university. In her quiet way she also branded into my soul a profound hatred of racism and injustice.

When I look back, given my family history it seems predetermined that I would become a civil rights lawyer and an activist in the Japanese Canadian redress movement. This belief was further confirmed when I began to go through family papers in preparation for this book. At my aunt's home in Hamilton I discovered my maternal grandmother's photo album. I've been told that this old collection is a rarity. In 1942, given a few hours' notice to relocate and limited to only one small suitcase per person, most practical-minded Japanese Canadians chose warm clothing over family keepsakes.

Knowing this, I treasure the sepia-coloured photos that tenuously connect me to my unfamiliar past. The album spans a forty-year period from the beginning of the twentieth century to the Second World War. Originally neatly catalogued with words written in a white Japanese script under each picture, the album is now in a sad state of repair with missing photographs and torn black pages. But staring out still are the stolid unsmiling faces of my grandmother's fairly prosperous family in Japan, most if not all of whom must certainly be dead by now. These strangers, whose names I do not know, represent one-quarter of my kin. I know nothing of the other three-quarters of my family.

I never met my father's parents, who after the war, had decided to remain in the B.C. interior. In those days, even with both my parents working and my older brother and sister helping out after school, there wasn't enough money to travel back west to visit them, in Kamloops. I know my father prayed for forgiveness all his life because he hadn't been able to attend his dad's funeral. And although he was curious, he never got the chance to visit Japan. By the time my father was in his seventies we had enough money to pay for his passage, but he said he was too old to go back. Perhaps too proud, he was afraid of being humiliated by boastful relatives who would laugh at his poverty. In his last years, my father's pride dictated that he prove that the years of struggle, hardship, and repression that he had endured in Canada had been worth it; that it hadn't all been in vain.

I am told that my father's mother was a tough tiny wisp of a woman who lived into her nineties. In her younger days she had been a travelling cloth peddler. Alone, in the years before the First World War, she would visit the various workcamps in and around Vancouver selling her wares. Over the years she hoarded her savings and bought property back in her home prefecture of Shiga-ken, in Japan. Given the sexism of my culture, I found her independence astonishing, at least until McGill professor and Montreal's representative on the NAJC's strategy-negotiation team, Audrey Kobayashi, explained her behaviour to me. According to Audrey, an authority on Japanese immigration to Canada, travel within Japan was severely restricted during the Tokugawa period (1590-1867). The island's feudal rulers only permitted some of the *Omi-shonin* (peddlers of Omi, the old name for Shiga prefecture, the home of my father's family) to move freely about the country. Later these peddlers became Japan's merchant class and entrepreneurs. In Canada many of the *Omi-shonin*, including my grandmother, set up stores on Powell Street in Vancouver's Japantown. Others became labour contractors and employment brokers. Custom permitted my grandmother to make her living in this fashion and tradition dictated that her fellow countrymen buy from her.

At war's end, faced with the government's ultimatum, my mother's entire family decided to move east. The only grandparent that I recall clearly is my mother's father. In Hamilton, for the first five years of my life, my maternal grandparents, various uncles, aunts, and cousins, together with my family, all lived in a three-storey brick house. The house, which had been painted fire-engine red, is still standing. It is located in the downtown north end, in an area that was frequented by the working poor, drunks and prostitutes. At that time it was also home to Japanese Canadians. As a young child I was forbidden to play on the street, and the house was my entire world. Filled with my extended family plus the occasional boarder, it nonetheless seemed spacious. Perhaps that was a result of the war years, when it had been common for two Japanese Canadian families – often with eight children between them – to live for years in a hut ten feet by twenty.

I remember that in the heat of the summer I would sometimes find my grandfather sitting in a chair down in the basement behind the furnace, drinking a cold beer. I was never sure if he was being punished for downing alcohol or whether he was trying to escape the censure and prying eyes of the women. But I knew that his whereabouts was a secret I shared with him.

I have a physical intolerance to alcohol inherited from my father, and although I am told that in Japan the Japanese are "drinkers," the Japanese Canadians I know rarely touch the stuff. My white husband laughs at my mother's stereotypical image of the *hakujin* as alcoholics. When he first began visiting my parents, my mother would immediately pull out a dusty bottle of scotch from the dark recesses of a cupboard and ask him if he wanted a drink, regardless of the time of day. With this attitude towards demon rum, it was no wonder that my grandfather took refuge in the basement. To a child my grandfather seemed a conspirator, always hiding out, in trouble with the adults. My mother had a special soft spot for him because, curious about the idiosyncrasies of the new world, he had always encouraged her to study and learn Canadian ways. In many respects my mother did the same with me.

In the early 1950s, my grandfather, against the wishes of his children, returned alone to his ancestral village of Kahogun, outside of Fukuoka on Japan's southern-most island, to build a large wooden house – a North American kind of house. He was determined to leave his mark, to prove his success. Back in the 1920s, together with his Japanese farm neighbours, he had constructed a two-storey wooden frame house in Haney, B.C. My grandfather planned that his Kahogun house would be a larger replica of the farmhouse where my mother had grown up.

In the decade after the war in bombed-out Japan, most people had no idea where their next meal was coming from, so my grandfather's relatives viewed their wiry Canadian kin as crazy. To dream of building an entirely new house constructed of wood, an expensive commodity – especially in a time when most of the locals were still clearing out rubble and making do – seemed the act of a madman. The family would not sanction the scheme and left him to hammer and nail by himself. The adventurous young boy who had escaped to northern British Columbia via Hawaii had returned to Japan as an old man, with not much more in his pockets. But still he was full of dreams and prepared to go it alone. One day, working on the roof of his new home, he collapsed and died of a massive heart attack.

Memories of my grandfather are few and incomplete. I am not certain if they are my own recollections or family folklore that I have absorbed. I lament the fact that I have no photos of my grandfather's family or his unfinished house in Japan. Perhaps if I had some mementos, I might know the man who would have been my rope bridge across the Pacific Ocean. In my search to link up the redress movement with our community's earlier activists and fighters, I was frustrated by death and dead ends. Knowing that the human memory is faulty and that stories get coloured in the telling, I nonetheless yearned to hear the past told by the living. So I turn to the only existing connection that I have to my ancestors, my grandmother's album. Flipping through the pages, I notice the consistently serious faces, as if the subjects believed the old superstition that a photograph could shorten their lives. I am struck by the snapshots of my mother as a child and teenager. How astoundingly beautiful she looks with her large dark eyes staring out from a face framed with thick straight hair.

In one adolescent photo my mother is wearing a coat with a fur-trimmed collar, looking very much like an adult. It reminds me of an old family story, of how my grandparents, illiterate in English, had given my mother the envied responsibility of ordering the family's yearly supply of clothes from the Eaton's catalogue. Having very little disposable income, these purchases were taken very seriously by each member of my mother's poor but self-sufficient farm family. One year when my mother was ordering her annual allotment of one pair of shoes, she secretly wrote down the number of a pair of fancy navy-blue suede high heels. Reality set in later on when she found herself making the daily trek to school along the miles of muddy country roads, hobbling in her pretty suede pumps. That, I suppose, is why as a child I was always forced to wear sturdy Buster Brown oxfords. Still, on my tenth birthday, my mother finally succumbed to my entreaties and agreed to buy me a pair of shiny black patent-leather shoes without laces. Perhaps she weakened, remembering those days.

Turning the pages of the album, I'm amazed by the bizarre photos of elaborately dressed Victorian women with Japanese faces. And I return again and again to a family portrait of great uncles, aunts, and cousins who are formally dressed in traditional Japanese kimonos, in front of what must be my ancestral home. I study the now-fading photos that document my grandmother's life at the turn of the century in British Columbia. There is only one wintery photo of Port Essington, a boom and bust fish cannery and lumbering town located at the mouth of the Skeena River, on the border where Canada ends and Alaska begins. Today the port is deserted and no longer exists. It was there for some reason that my grandfather first settled and where my mother was born.

The adjustment to life in frontier Canada must have been hard on my grandmother. In addition to the unfamiliar cold – she had come from southern Japan which has a climate similar to that of southern California – my grandmother felt lonely and isolated in rough northern British Columbia, where it rained six months of the year. As soon as he could, my grandfather and the entire Japanese colony in Port Essington, probably on the urging of their wives, moved south to the sunny fertile Fraser Valley, where life proved to be no less difficult, though considerably less harsh. There was land to clear, there were homes to build, and they had to face the daily backbreaking field labour of the market and berry farmer. But they could call it their own and there were better educational opportunities for the children. It seemed a fitting place to build a future.

It was there, in Haney, B.C., that my mother grew up and where my grandparents farmed for almost thirty years – until 1942, when they were forced to relocate, ironically enough, to northern British Columbia. The Haney photographs portray the rich social life of a small insular community. My grandmother was active in the Japanese women's association and the women's auxiliary of the Buddhist church. Her album contains pictures of her family, her best friends, and their children, as well as of the community weddings, funerals, and church socials. Amid the photos are pictures of my grandmother with her girlfriends. Astonishingly, I have discovered that one of these women was the grandmother of Art Miki, the president of the NAJC, and his brother Roy, one of the principal organizers in Vancouver; and another was of the great aunt of Audrey Kobayashi, a leader in the Montreal Japanese Canadian community. Four of the six redress negotiators can trace their roots back to these women.

My Hamilton aunt recalls that my grandmother and her chums declared January their month because there was no work to be done then on the farms. They would gather up their youngest children and move in with one another, spending the time sewing and enjoying each other's company. In the 1940s the three families were removed from the Fraser Valley and scattered across the country, from Vancouver to Montreal. Yet somehow, two generations later, we who had previously been strangers to one another were brought together through the redress movement.

Although my grandparents lived with my family until I was five, I have few recollections of my pioneer grandmother. Yet I am sure that she is secretly pleased that her grandchild and the grandchildren of her friends helped lay to rest the wartime injustice done to our community.

Art Miki (front row, left) and his family in Ste. Agathe, Manitoba sugar-beet field, 1942.

3 | Yamato-Damashii versus the Lesson of the Bamboo

We could not forget,
Nor yet go back to Japan.
Without our homeland
Most of us Issei were like
Trees that were slowly dying.

– Kimiko Ono, an issei immigrant[1]

IN MY SEARCH for an understanding of the first-generation Japanese Canadians, issei, and their history in this country, I stumbled again and again across the imagery of *Yamato-damashii*. *Yamato*, among other things, can mean "peace", "harmony", or "warrior", as well as being the original name for Japan. *Damashii* means "spirit."

Yamato-damashii – with all its various meanings and implications – goes back to an ancient folk tale about Yamato, the son of twelfth emperor Keiko, who ruled from 71 to 130 A.D. At the age of twenty-two Yamato was sent on a mission by his father to Kyushu, the large island in the southern part of the archipelago, to kill ruthless bandits who were terrorizing the region. Disguising himself as a beautiful woman, Yamato lured the robbers into a cave and slaughtered them with his sword, ripping them apart "like ripe melons." Over a ten-year period Yamato travelled throughout the land, subduing warring princes in the south and the "barbarous Ainu" in the far north. Putting their territories under the control of his father, he consolidated the nation. According to legend, peace and harmony prevailed throughout the country.

In one of the battles, in the middle of a terrible storm, Yamato's wife, Azuma, threw herself overboard as an offering to the fierce sea gods to save her husband from certain death. Shortly thereafter Yamato, suffering from the loss of his beloved and beautiful wife, died under a pine tree while romantically composing a poem to her.[2] Not surprisingly, for the Japanese the story of Yamato has long symbolized the idealized virtues of filial duty, bravery, and heroism, making Yamato in romanticized versions of Japanese history a figure similar in stature to Ullyses in western mythology.

When they arrived in North America the nineteenth-century Japanese pioneers, poetically described as *kaitakusha*– translated literally as "those who part the grass" – brought the legend with them in their collective memory. It provided them with the psychological stamina to withstand the heart-grinding loneliness and the soul-destroying discrimination that were oftentimes their daily lot.[3] Indeed, as Canadian historians such as Ken Adachi and Yayashi indicate, the issei tended to invoke this name – Yamato – whenever they became embroiled in a difficult struggle with outside forces.

Like other age-old civilizations, Japan's collective memory contains elements from both its own past and mythology, and the adopted ideas and finery of others. But Japan's history of relations with the outside world has generally been one of selective quarantine and exclusion.

For Japan, the seventh and eighth centuries marked a great "borrowing period."[4] With total abandon the island's cultural soul absorbed China at its shining peak. However, more than a millennium would pass before Japan would again open itself to the influence of *gaijin*, or foreigners. By the end of the sixteenth century Japan was increasingly trading and colonizing in the South Pacific.[5] As a seafaring nation with expansionist policies, the Japanese came into contact with the Spaniards, and in 1610 and 1613 the island's rulers sent envoys to Acapulco, Mexico, to study trade possibilities with New Spain.[6] The *Mayflower* had not yet landed at Plymouth.

By 1638 this brief association with Europeans was enough to convince the nation's monarchs, the Tokugawa Shoguns, to close the island to further foreign influence. This monastic seclusion was compounded by a strictly enforced regulation that prohibited Japanese nationals from leaving the country under pain of death.

The seeds of my own fate were sown in the mid-1850s when U.S. gunboats militarily forced Japan out of its two-hundred-year-old self-imposed isolation. Japan, like its Asian neighbours, was battling Western powers who were scrambling amongst themselves to carve up the "Far East." The British were in Hong Kong, the Dutch in the East Indies, the Portuguese in Macao and Timor, the Spanish in the Philippines, and the French in the Pacific islands. In 1867 the United States bought Alaska and the Aleutian Islands and acquired the Midway islands in the North Pacific. While Japan struggled to retain its sovereignty, it was simultaneously involved in imperialist ventures of its own. In the great land grab of the period, Japan was countering Russian forays into the island of Sakhalin (still the site of a dispute between the two countries) and maintaining its control of Manchuria and Korea, territories that Japan had claimed for itself.[7]

The year 1867 marked both Canada's founding and the end of Japan's regime of isolationism. Political power returned to Emperor Meiji and the Imperial throne. During the forty-five years of the Meiji reign, Japan entered the country's second "borrowing period," this time opening itself widely to Western ideas and technology. Rapidly, in great leaps and bounds, Japan industrialized and westernized. By 1900, the island's population had increased to forty-four million people and had undergone the radical social metamorphosis from a feudal to an industrial society. Like the British experience, this change was borne at great hardship by the many sectors of the population who became the fodder for cannons and colonial expansion.

Still, influences from the West brought about indisputable advances as well: the spread of modern medicine, the elimination of former caste restrictions, and a rapid increase in literacy.[8] By 1912 ninety-eight per cent of the country's children were attending school.[9] With the ending of the socially repressive Meiji regime there was a brief period, during the "Taisho Democracy" (1912-26) when Western democratic and revolutionary ideas and politics flourished.

With the coming of those U.S. gunboats, Meiji-Taisho Japan was pried open like a clam. Merchants, students, and immigrants were once again permitted to travel abroad. From 1868 to 1875, eleven hundred Japanese travelled to Europe and North America as students/explorers. In 1868, one hundred and fifty Japanese contract labourers emigrated to Hawaii to toil on sugar plantations where Japanese and Chinese coolies worked in near-slave conditions. Paternalistically, the Japanese government discouraged further immigration to the Hawaiian islands. From 1869 to 1884 another 15,416 people left Japan, primarily for China and Korea, though many of them returned home after finding lower living standards abroad. By 1885 the Meiji government had negotiated a treaty with Hawaiian sugar planters allowing the emigration of a further nine hundred Japanese labourers. My maternal grandfather, an adventurous teenage boy at the time, was one of them.

By the 1890s Japanese immigrants started to come to Canada in larger numbers for the first time, although most Japanese still preferred to make their way to the United States. In 1907 the Americans, anxious to stem the flood of the "yellow hordes," amended a regulation that had previously permitted "Orientals" from Hawaii to continue onto the mainland. As a result, more Japanese emigrated to Canada in 1907 than in any other year past or present.

The Russo-Japanese war of 1904-05 had just ended with Japan's defeat of Russia – the first time a non-white state had beaten a white nation. Japan's stature rose in the international community, and the results were to be felt even in Canada. Treaties were ultimately signed that granted, among other things, the right of citizens of the signator countries to migrate and settle in each other's territories. The British-Japanese alliance explains why the Canadian colonial government treated Japanese immigrants better than those from China or India. Before 1907, Japanese migrants had been primarily seasonal male labourers granted three-year travel visas to leave Japan. But from 1907 to 1920, wives were allowed to join their mates and the Japanese communities in North America slowly began to put down roots.

Whites in Australia, the United States, and Canada responded by setting up rabid anti-Asian organizations. Political reaction followed quickly. Australia passed a whites-only policy. On July 1, 1924, the U.S. government closed the door to Asian immigration. Canada was hamstrung because as a British colony it was bound by the 1894 terms of the

Treaty of Commerce and Navigation and the Anglo-Japanese Treaty of 1905 that acknowledged Japan's special status as a British naval ally. By 1928, though, after a series of court battles, Canada was able to assert control over its own immigration policy. [10] Reading the writing on the wall in North America, Japan turned its focus to South America. Between 1908 to 1924, 48,182 Japanese were permitted to emigrate to Brazil, Peru, and Argentina.

At the beginning of the twentieth century, Japan's rulers had hoped that emigration would ease the country's problems of high population growth, overcrowding, and unemployment. But since emigration from Japan to all countries totalled about twenty thousand in the best years and those who returned numbered around fourteen thousand a year, the net outflow was limited. [11] Other answers had to be found, and among them would be the push towards industrialization, increased trade and imperialism, and eventually militarism. From their first arrival in Canada in 1877, the issei were universally treated as second-class citizens and regarded as members of an inferior race. But the issei – those who parted the grass – met the solid wall of white emnity with the comforting mythological belief that they had come from a land that was the offspring of two gods, Izanagi and Izanami, and from a people who through Jimmu, the first emperor, claimed direct descent from the sun goddess Amaterasu.

In their minds a chosen people, the issei were filled with indomitable pride in themselves. They wore this talisman as they toiled at the backbreaking labour of the fisher, the homestead farmer, the coal miner, and the logger. They passed this secret amulet to their children and encouraged them to work hard. Deep inside, the issei believed that they would succeed in North America in spite of the great odds against them. In 1907 the issei called upon this faith to repulse a huge and violent crowd of white hooligans in Vancouver. An angry mob of some five thousand racists, feeling threatened by increasing emigration from China and Japan and fired up by speeches advocating a "White Canada," moved through Chinatown breaking windows and looting. Taken by surprise, the Chinese offered no resistance. However as the rabble swept into Little Tokyo they found an eery stillness and utter darkness: all of the lights in the community had been extinguished. Suddenly, from the rooftops of both sides of the street the racists were pelted with a shower of rocks. As Ken Adachi described it, the Japanese "sallied forth with sticks, clubs, iron bars, knives and bottles. Crying 'Banzai' they tore into the mob." The invaders "soon wavered, broke, retreated ... their lust for conflict quickly dissipated by the unexpected and fiery resistance."[12] By nightfall the Japanese had organized their own patrols to protect the quarter. Japanese sentries were relieved at the end of their shift, and Little Toyko was ablaze with lights so intruders could be easily spotted. Several days later arsonists set the Japanese language school on Alexander Street ablaze, but the fire was quickly put out.

The Chinese began to purchase guns and ammunition and embarked on an unofficial strike. The Japanese staged a half-day sit-down and held a mass meeting at the language school. Tempers began to cool by the week's end. A year later, in 1908, Canada and Japan entered into a "Gentlemen's Agreement" (drafted in part by William Lyon Mackenzie King), whereby Japanese emigration to Canada was limited to four hundred people a year. This annual figure would remain fairly constant for the remainder of this century.

Although the gangs of ruffians were repulsed in a grand gesture of self-defence, it was a Pyrrhic victory at best. With an accord to severely restrict immigration it seemed only a matter of time before the Japanese Canadian community would disappear. In the 1940s the Canadian government's policy of repression and dispersal would be the final blow to the community's hopes for survival.

I can recall the times, as a child sitting in my father's lap, when he would tell me to have pride in myself and in my heritage. He tried to inoculate me against the self-hatred that silently infects the immigrant children of this land. Yet, ironically, when I discussed the Yamato legend with colleagues from Japan, their initial reaction was one of horror. For they had been raised as members of a chauvinistic racial majority in Japan, and not as a discriminated against minority. They associated the glorification of Yamato with racism, imperialism, and militarism. They advised me to bury the myth. I could not follow their counsel. From the very outset, racial bigotry followed my community like a shadow. Here in Canada, the anglos had invoked the full force of WASP legend to justify their rule. Oppressed Japanese Canadians needed to hang onto the Yamato amulet to help ensure their spiritual and physical survival.

Much of our history in this country has been a record of a solitary and difficult battle for equal rights. This struggle was oftentimes waged by a handful of men and women who not only faced the hatred of the white majority but also, sad to say, the derision and disapproval of their own community. These Japanese idealists had to combat not only the virulent white Anti-Asiatic League, but also the Japanese Association, which was dominated by the Japanese consul and Japanese Canadian businessmen. The overwhelming majority of the issei were traditionalists, who respected authority, whether it was the Emperor, his consul, or the government of Mackenzie King. Unless pushed into a corner that allowed no saving of face they were willing to accept their second-class status in Canada with Confucian fatalism— shikataga-nai.

The issei had come from a country in which community institutions had attained a high degree of co-ordinated efficiency. In Japan no town or village was without its customary associations formed by various age and sex groups, and most occupations had some organized form of representation. Every little village had its local council where group decisions were made. So in Canada the Japanese also banded together into fishing, farming, and lumber co-ops. They carried on the ancient tradition of tonari gumi, or working together. Drawing on this background proved a source of great stability and provided a sense of social value and protection. By 1934 Canadian officials were surprised to discover that there were 230 religious and secular associations for the small, recently established Japanese minority. [13] At times the leaders of these organizations were far-sighted men who encouraged their members to demand parity with whites and who saw the community's long-term interests as being tied to those of white working men and women in Canada— and not to relatives in villages in Japan. [14]

One of the very first of these men was Tomey Homma, a descendant of the samurai class who had immigrated to Canada in 1887 at the age of twenty-two. Homma, an intellectual and life-long community activist, was one of the founders of the fishermen's union, newspaper, community hospital, and Japanese language school in Steveston, B.C. In those days, Steveston was the centre of the Japanese fishing industry; today it is a Vancouver suburb. Homma later established a Vancouver Japanese daily, the Canada Shimpo, which was the most conservative of three daily Japanese language papers serving the Vancouver community.

Eight years after Homma's arrival in Canada, in 1895, the B.C.

government enacted section eight of the B.C. Elections Act, denying the vote to all Asians: immigrants from China, Japan and India. This exclusion included not only naturalized first-generation immigrants but also, significantly, their Canadian-born children. The white provincial legislators apparently feared that the growing number of Asians would "distort" the results of an election; or, as the Victoria *Colonist* put it, they feared "the possibility of having polling booths swamped by a horde of Orientals who are totally unfitted either by custom or education to exercise the ballot, and whose voting would completely demoralise politics."[15]

Far-sightedly realizing the serious implications of this legislation, Homma decided to challenge it in the courts. In 1900 he applied to have his name added to the Vancouver voters' list. When polling officer Thomas Cunningham refused, Homma appealed to the B.C. courts. When Homma was successful at the first level, the B.C. government appealed the decision to the Supreme Court of Canada, and again Homma won. Angered by this judgment, the provincial government took Homma's victory to the Privy Council in England, which in 1903 reversed the decisions of the Canadian courts and upheld the 1895 B.C. Act. The Privy Council ruled that the B.C. government and not the federal government had the right to determine who could vote in provincial elections.

In effect the 1895 B.C. Elections Act created a subclass of citizens who were denied the vote, the right to hold public office, or the right to serve on juries, all on the basis of their race. Provincial voting legislation also severely curtailed employment opportunities. Effectively Japanese were unable to work on timber leases, log on crown lands, receive government contracts, work as school teachers, underground miners, and provincial or municipal civil servants. They were also unable to enter professions such as law or pharmacy.[16] Slowly the community's few remaining open doors were being padlocked shut. Almost exclusively, the issei were being funnelled into farming, logging, and fishing. When they started to prosper in those occupations, whites began lobbying to drive them out.

By 1900 the Japanese had obtained almost half of the province's issued fishing licences, and whites were feeling threatened. An undeclared "battle" for survival was begun, with the issei "prepared to die if necessary" during fishing "wars" that came to dominate the early years of the century.[17] The battle to maintain white control over west coast fishing continued unabated. Leaping off the pages of Adachi's history were powerful images of: shotgun-carrying company thugs; the reading of the "Riot Act" and the calling in of the militia to quell the rampages; the unexplained deaths of Japanese fishermen; mass demonstrations in the streets of Steveston by four thousand Japanese fishers; and the arming of the Japanese fishermen.[18] The events struck a match to the racial oil slick that covered B.C.'s Pacific shoreline.

Reading Adachi, my heart and mind raced. It sounded like a familiar movie script, but wrongly cast with my relatives. Impossible to conceive. What was this *Yamato-damashii*, I wondered as I examined the faces of the oldest in our community who had lived through those years. How could those lined faces and tiny withered bodies have housed such fearlessness?

The white fishermen fought the combat on two fronts: to drive the Japanese out of fishing and to bargain for better prices from the canneries. The cannery owners used the very presence of the Japanese fishers to weaken the militancy of the whites. For its part, bowing to the white lobby, the B.C. government refused to renew the fishing licences of the Japanese Canadians, leaving thousands of them without a livelihood. In 1923 the Steveston Japanese Farmers' Co-operative was organized to help the jobless fishermen transfer from old to new ventures. The Co-op bought eighty acres of land, which it rented on an instalment basis to unemployed fishers. The Co-op then organized a series of classes to teach these former fishers "the rudiments of Occidental farming."[19] The thinking was, "We do not wish to see our own 'ken' (prefecture) people starving or committing a crime, for in either case it reflects disgrace on us. If he is starving, we should take responsibility for helping him, and if he displays any criminal tendencies, we should restrain him and lead him back to proper conduct."[20]

The race-war in the fishing industry lasted until the mid-1930s, by which time most of the Japanese had been pushed out of the industry.

Soon after I hung out my shingle and started practice as a young idealistic lawyer, I read the biography of Ryuichi Yoshida, a principal organizer of the Japanese fishermen's union.[21] I remember the excitement I felt: here was the first Japanese Canadian I had come upon who had devoted his life to combatting racism and injustice. Yoshida, trained in law in Japan, had lived in Canada as a jack of all trades – a fisher, logger, trade unionist, journalist, and steelworker. At times he was reviled and blacklisted by the powerful within the Japanese Canadian community. This man, who lived in poverty and had few material possessions, became my Japanese working-class hero. To me, his dynamic fighting ways and deep convictions epitomized the best in the human spirit.

I was surprised to learn that after the war Yoshida had moved to my hometown of Hamilton to begin work at the age of sixty in the punishing steel-coke ovens. In 1952, at the age of sixty-five, his health broken, he returned with his wife to New Denver, a small town in the B.C. interior, where he had probably spent his internment years. I was further surprised to be told that during the five years he had lived in Hamilton, Yoshida had rented an apartment on Mary Street in the city's gritty core, one block from the house where I had first grown up. Perhaps as a young child I had seen the big, white-haired old man with the large rough hands of a worker at the Hamilton Japanese Canadian community picnics and festivals.

I was moved when I read that, although Yoshida had hoped through his struggles to improve the working conditions of his fellow countrymen in British Columbia, at the end of his life he believed he had accomplished nothing, and he felt "empty." Knowing that my hero would by then be eighty-nine years of age, I hurriedly dashed off a letter to him, explaining the pride I had felt in reading his selfless story. For weeks I waited for a reply, but none ever came.

It was distressing to find out that my community had often reviled and ostracized firebrands like Yoshida. Others included organizers such as John Kumaji Nihei, who worked as a shipping clerk in an Ocean Falls pulp mill, and was a member of the *rodo-kumiai*, a labour group engaging in political debate, social criticism, and organized activism. Like others in his circle, Nihei fought for equal pay for equal work. In those days Japanese – if they were lucky enough to be hired – were paid only about half as much as whites, and they usually got the worst jobs to do.[22] Nihei's daughter Jean still remembers bitterly how stigmatized she felt throughout her adolescence, being the daughter of an *aka* (a red). Jean was to become a stalwart member of the Vancouver redress committee.

By all accounts, Etsu Suzuki was one of the most charismatic Japanese to cross the ocean: he was a forceful orator, a leading intellectual, and an effective trade union organizer. In 1924 Suzuki founded a left-wing Japanese daily in Vancouver called the *Minshu* (People). His wife, Toshiko Tamura, a popular Meiji novelist, was perhaps the most famous Japanese woman to emigrate to Canada. Fleeing failed marriages in Tokyo, they had both escaped to Vancouver.

Tamura later wrote a book entitled *Love in Vancouver* that describes Suzuki and the turbulent 1920s in British Columbia.[23] A sophisticated woman, Tamura flaunted the religious and social mores of the Vancouver Japantown backwater that she found herself in. A feminist of sorts, she promoted social dancing, public speaking for women, and birth control. With her flapper's haircut and liberated ways, Toshiko Tamura was the centre of scandal and envy. In Japan, Suzuki and Tamura had been members of the Tokyo intelligentsia. In Canada they continued to lead a nonconformist bohemian life that shocked the hard-working, almost puritanical issei. They were the centre of a small coterie of Japanese Canadians in the *rodo-kumiai*.

Kay Kato Shimizu's parents were members of the same social circle. Today Kay, a feisty feminist nisei in her seventies and our community's first social worker, still remembers Toshiko Tamura. Kay's mother, a friend of Tamura's, sought to pattern herself after the Tokyo free-thinker. Kay's father, Yomishi Kato, was injured in a logging accident and devoted much of his life to organizing Japanese fishers and loggers. Kay remembers the gatherings held at her parents' home where men such as Suzuki and Yoshida discussed the exploitation and oppression faced by Japanese workers and planned strategies for winning equality with whites through unionization. Partly out of ideology and partly out of necessity, the Katos lived in a "long house," where five or six Japanese families rented separate sleeping quarters but shared a communal kitchen, bathroom, laundry, and social areas. Kay remembers that there were always kids to play with and mothers to oversee the activities. Most of the fathers were seasonal labourers and away for months at a time, so the living arrangement provided stability and company for the women and children.

Kay's parents were illiterate in English, and from the early age of ten she got used to going with them to endless union and political meetings to act as their translator. Excluded from white unions, Etsu Suzuki and his followers set out to organize the unorganized Japanese into one union. These issei heroes were leading a struggle to gain the franchise, better working conditions, and higher wages. Organizing was difficult, though, because most of the Japanese were economic migrants who saw Canada simply as a temporary paycheque. With no emotional commitment to stay, they had little incentive to accommodate themselves to Canadian society. By 1918, like birds of passage, some seventy-five per cent of the migrants had gone back to their ancestoral villages in Japan, taking their hard-earned savings with them. These first-born sons returned to Japan to inherit the family properties and fulfil their filial duties to care for their aging parents. Most of the issei who planned one day to leave Canada had a conservative, authoritarian worldview and looked for leadership from the Japanese consul-general, who acted as an intermediary between the immigrant community and the Canadian government. In the end these men felt that it was easier to ignore the daily humiliations and injustices.

It was their younger brothers, who had no family obligations and only small inheritances to return to, who made the decision to remain in Canada, and who formed what would be the backbone of the Japanese Canadian community. They naively believed that if they became model Canadians, the government would see the error of its ways and become more supportive of their rights. But still, within the community, as in Canada itself, populist and socialist ideas were hotly debated. About ninety-eight per cent of the first-generation immigrants were literate in Japanese, and given their national penchant for reading most of them subscribed to more than one of the three Japanese-language dailies, in which debates over democratic rights were being aired. [24]

By the late 1930s labour peace, and some equality, did seem to be more of a possibility. *The Fisherman*, the official newspaper of the all-white United Fishermen and Allied Workers Union (UFAWU), began publishing editorials attacking previously held racist and anti-Japanese views and began urging co-operation with the Japanese fishermen's union. In 1941 Takaichi Umezuki, who at the time held the position of secretary of the Japanese Canadian Camp and Mill Workers Union, wrote that *The Fisherman*'s editorials had been translated and reprinted in one of Vancouver's Japanese-language newspapers, where it had created a "very favorable reaction amongst Japanese workers." [25]

Umezuki added that "the burning question confronting the Japanese community today is the need for unity and co-operation of the entire working classes, regardless of nationality, color or political belief." Umezuki, a disciple of Etsu Suzuki, worked on Suzuki's labour daily, the *Minshu*, and was later to become the Japanese publisher of *The New Canadian*, the first English-language Japanese Canadian newspaper. During the Second World War, when all Japanese papers were closed down, the federal government permitted only *The New Canadian* to continue publishing, under the editorship of nisei Tom Shoyama.

In 1939 a twenty-three-year-old nisei fisherman, Buck Suzuki, was invited to address the Pacific Coast Fisherman's Union on the topic of building bridges between the Japanese and the whites. Buck Suzuki was a perfect choice. Born on Don Island on the south arm of the Fraser River, the son of a fisherman, Suzuki had obtained his commercial fishing licence at the age of nine. During the Second World War he served in the Canadian armed forces stationed in India, Ceylon, and Singapore. As a veteran, Buck was granted permission to take his family back to Vancouver in March 1947, but it wasn't until 1949 that he was able to return to his first love, fishing. In 1951, two years after the lifting of all restrictions against Japanese Canadians, at the age of thirty-five, Buck Suzuki was elected to the executive of the UFAWU. Buck was to serve eleven terms as union vice-president, one year as acting president, and two years as welfare director. The UFAWU named its environmental foundation after Buck in recognition of his life-long concern for the environment.

Unfortunately for the Japanese Canadian community, Etsu Suzuki, a key political and intellectual leader of the issei, returned to Japan in 1931. Perhaps Suzuki returned to Tokyo to combat the rising power of the Japanese militarists who were rounding up and arresting their leftist political opponents. As in Germany in the same period, the Japanese right-wing was silencing all opposition to its imperialist views. In fact, between 1931 and 1933, 45,722 members of the Japanese Communist Party were arrested and imprisoned and no doubt countless more supporters of the Japanese Socialist Party met a similar fate.[26] Their enemies removed, the militarists successfully manoeuvred Japan onto a course for war. Tremors would soon be felt not only in Southeast Asia but also within the unsuspecting Japanese Canadian community on British Columbia's west coast.

Tragically, Suzuki was never to return to Canada. He died in 1932 in Japan. Toshiko Tamura, depressed by the news, followed her husband

and returned to Japan. She died in Manchuria at the war's end. On occasion I like to speculate what kind of a role Suzuki might have played during the 1940s in Canada. But then it is probably naive to think that one man could have made a difference. In the Japanese Canadian community the idealists were the exception and not the rule, and in any case the fragile alliances that they were developing with whites were ruptured by the bombing of Pearl Harbour.

In 1936 a dispute erupted in the House of Commons as to whether or not "Orientals" should get the vote – or even as to whether they wanted it. A CCF Member of Parliament, Angus MacInnis, long a supporter of Japanese Canadians and their right to the franchise, contacted the Japanese Canadian Citizens League (JCCL) in Vancouver and invited a delegation to appear before the Special Committee on Elections and Franchise Acts of the House of Commons. Quickly the Vancouver community organized a meeting, which determined that the representatives to this hearing could not be the issei, who had little command of English. For their part, the issei doubted whether a contingent led by their children could be trusted with such an important task. Still others feared a white backlash. Nonetheless, at a subsequent public gathering resistance evaporated and the community decided to send a nisei contingent to Ottawa to lobby for the franchise. A fundraising campaign was launched, no easy task in the midst of the Depression.

Hide Hyodo Shimizu, a nisei in Steveston, was asked if she would join the Ottawa delegation. Hide, the community's first accredited teacher, now in her eighties, laughingly recalls that in those days women were not included in discussions – they were "just hauled in when they were needed." But the JCCL thought one of the four delegates should be a woman because, Hide says, this would help "influence the *hakujin*." The other members were Edward Banno, a Vancouver dentist, Minoru Kobayashi, a Steveston insurance salesman, and Professor Isamu Hayakawa, who was later to become a U.S. senator and, ironically, a major opponent of Japanese American redress.

On their train trip east the four delegates intently studied in preparation for their presentation before the House of Commons committee. On May 22, 1936, each of them got fifteen minutes to make the case for extending voting rights to Japanese Canadians. They were taunted and peppered with questions from two anti-Asian MPs with broad Scottish accents that Hide found difficult to understand. In the end, even though Hayakawa presented a rousing quotation from the Scottish poet Robbie Burns, the committee decided against extending the vote to Japanese Canadians.

On June 5, 1936, after the delegation's return to Vancouver, Hide and the others told a packed public meeting of three hundred people of their failure. Disappointed, the community silently filed out of the Japanese language school. Although the franchise ban also included Canadians of Chinese and Indian ancestry, at the time those minorities were even more impoverished and powerless than the Japanese. Although Japanese Canadians were advised by the CCF to continue to pressure the House of Commons, Hide Shimizu's group was the last important delegation the community would send to Ottawa for almost fifty years.

This exclusion from the franchise was hurtful to the Japanese Canadian community in more ways than one. In 1921, for instance, the B.C. Pharmaceutical Association amended the Pharmacy Act to require that all students or apprentices to the profession be registered on the provincial voters' list. But some Japanese Canadians persevered. Despite the restriction, in the early 1920s Tahe Niimi and his son Toragoro purchased the Isshi drugstore at 331 Powell Street. The Niimis ran their drugstore for twenty years, selling non-prescription patent drugs and Japanese herbal medicines. Notwithstanding the professional ban, and perhaps with the hope that the Provincial Elections Act would one day be amended to give the rights of citizenship to Canadian-born Japanese, Tahe had sent his second son Joe to Washington State University to study pharmacy. Joe graduated in the early 1930s.

Joe Niimi soon discovered that the provincial legislature, despite pressure from the Trades and Labour Congress of Canada, had no intention of granting the rights of citizenship to Canadian-born Japanese. Unable to practise, Joe was forced to leave his family and emigrate to Japan to make use of his training. In 1942, like all Japanese Canadians, the Niimis were forced to leave their home and store and move to the B.C. interior.

At the end of the 1940s, with the barriers finally crumbling, Tahe Niimi's grandson Peter enrolled in the school of pharmacy at the University of British Columbia. When Peter graduated in the early 1950s he was the first Japanese Canadian to do so. Even then finding a place to complete his apprenticeship was difficult, but he finished his training on Powell Street, in the old Japanese quarter, serving with a former competitor of his grandfather and father. By the 1990s Peter Niimi owned four drugstores, and his son, David, the great-grandson of Tahe Niimi, had also graduated from U.B.C. in pharmacy.

A year after the redress settlement, I was reminded of the Niimis when I passed their old store on my way to Vancouver's Stanley Park. Once the Niimi name had been set in red inlay in the stone pavement in front of the Powell Street store. Now it is gone. That day, entering Vancouver's Stanley Park under a grey sky threatening rain, my feet sank into the lushness of fall grass after a week's deluge. I had come to join several dozen Japanese Canadians for a Remembrance Day service. The morning's stillness was broken by the sharp cries of Canada geese, fleetingly visible overhead in the patches of sky that I could see through the tree branches.

A group of us stood around the thirty-four-foot white sandstone column with its marble Japanese lantern on top. The memorial had been erected in 1920 to commemorate the fifty-four Japanese Canadians who had died in World War I, but for years it had been allowed to deteriorate. In the mid-1980s Vancouver's Japanese Canadian community had petitioned the provincial government to restore the monument and rekindle the flame. High above us the light at the very top flickered.

Now, in my forties, I am still unable to wear a poppy. My mind contains too many memories of being the token enemy alien during the Remembrance Day ceremonies that took place in the Hamilton school gymnasiums and auditoriums of my youth. I recall my feelings of shame and embarrassment as I felt a hundred pairs of eyes boring little holes in my back during those annual patriotic displays. I knew that many of the old white men being honoured on stage with their navy blue berets and shiny medals harboured thoughts favouring my people's genocide at Hiroshima or Nagasaki. Yet at this particular Remembrance Day service, recognizing those Japanese Canadians who had died for their adopted country in the First and Second World Wars, I felt strangely moved. I recalled my unknown benefactors who had been prepared to sacrifice everything for the rights of Canadian citizenship. This purpose was stated explicitly in the 1916 Constitution of the Japanese Canadian Overseas Volunteers, which read: "These 200 men go not only as soldiers to fight in the Canadian war. They go to sacrifice themselves in the battle to achieve rights here at home.... The question of franchise in B.C. is still not settled. The sacrifice of these men is to break this barrier."

The World War I record speaks for itself: 197 Japanese Canadian volunteers, 131 wounded in action, and 54 killed in action. To support the war effort the Canadian government had asked the Japanese Canadian community to raise $50,000 in victory bonds, and the small community had greatly exceeded its quota, raising $235,400. In 1919, at a special civic luncheon held in Vancouver, the community received the Prince of Wales flag in recognition of its support. Speaking for the community, Mr. S. Ukita said that during the war the Japanese were prepared to sacrifice their lives if necessary for the king and country of their adoption. "We are prepared to finish the job now. We realize that we are real Canadians, and that we must help our country. This is the spirit which is carrying us on, and we will continue in our work."[27]

Despite repeated promises, it wasn't until April 1, 1931, by a vote of nineteen to eighteen, that the B.C. politicians honoured their pledge and granted the franchise to the approximately one hundred and forty surviving Japanese Canadian veterans. It would be almost two more decades before the vote was extended to all Japanese Canadians. But the decades of slow, spirit-breaking racism that culminated in the total repression of the 1940s was not without its effect. It bent the proud pioneer toughness of the issei and reinforced the push of their children, the nisei, towards assimilation and the *shikataga-nai* (resigned) outlook.

From the beginning, within the bosom of the community the spirit of *Yamato-damashii* has been at war with the prevailing values of *enryo* (reserve, restraint), *gamen* (patience, perseverance), and most importantly *shikataga-nai* (fatalistic resignation). But it was the events of the 1940s that caused the triumph of *shikataga-nai*. The wartime trauma of the internment camps, the loss of property, the mass deportations to Japan, and the forced dispersals across the country psychologically dispirited the majority of Japanese Canadians to the point of passivity. If we became proud of anything it was our invisibility and low crime rate as we tried ever harder to assimilate. Afraid to draw attention to ourselves, Japanese Canadians presented a contrast to other Asian Canadians. I remember when I was growing up I often wanted to disappear into thin air whenever Chinese immigrants boarded the bus. Invariably they would shout in Chinese to one another as if they were still back home conversing across rice fields. Hadn't they learned, I wondered, that in public Canadians acted as if they didn't even know their own mothers? No escape: with my slanted eyes and coloured skin I too was visibly part of that great yellow peril. Perhaps that explains why throughout my school years I was nagged by my teachers to speak up. I had slit my tongue.

In those days it was commonly thought that my race could only copy white ideas. As a child growing up in the 1950s I felt bereft of ethnic heroes. If only in hindsight, my mother had read me the stories of the warrior prince Yamato instead of the endless fables counselling endurance of suffering and the obeying of elders' orders. Typical of those Japanese legends is the story of Hoichi, the blind *biwa* player.[28] Bewitched by ghosts, Hoichi was saved for all time when he followed the advice of the temple priests to stoically withstand one night of inhuman torture to be inflicted upon him by the devils. To protect Hoichi the priests inscribed the words of a holy Buddhist sutra on every part of his body except, through an oversight, on his ears. The sutra was the "Doctrine of the Emptiness of Forms" – that nothing exists, including pain.[29] In the morning a frightened Hoichi was found by the priests, minus his ears, which had been pulled off by the evil spirits.

In those days, Hoichi-like, my parents cautioned moderation. My mother worried when I became politically active in the late 1960s, predicting darkly that the RCMP would "come and take me away." I perceived my community and therefore myself as cowardly. If not, then why were we called yellow-bellied? How else to explain that as a child I would run away from the school bully as he hurled racist abuse at me, rather than stay and fight? Why had I never even thought to ask my big sister to beat him up?

Perhaps, I thought, it was genetic. After all, my grandparents had endured second-class status and my parents had allowed themselves, without a protest, to be stripped not only of their property but also of their freedom and dignity. I felt humiliated and betrayed by my weary father and uncles who were too busy trying to put food on the table to worry about lofty ideals or cultural genocide. It was the nisei, my parents' generation, who had best learned the "lesson of the bamboo": bend with the wind and you will not be broken; bend with the force and absorb its energy. But my discovery of the valiant fighters in our past explains my pride in learning that we weren't always this way. It also helps me to understand that our passivity was fashioned by our history in this country, that, like some invisible undertow, pulls us down on bended knees.

Vancouver, Summer 1945. (Left to right): Tom Shoyama, President, JCCA, 1948, George Tanaka, Secretary, JCCA, 1947–1953, Roger Obata, President, JCCA, 1947.

4 | War Stories

In leaving B.C.,
we left family and friends.
Many were reunited but it was not the same.
Nor will it ever be the same.
And in going forward we tried
with many a backward glance to keep in sight
all that we held dear to our hearts.
The time comes when we must lose
the last link to these too,
and until the moment when one takes
the last step into oblivion,
one remembers the sound of fading footsteps,
the quiet sadness of a silent farewell.

– Muriel Kitagawa 1946,[1]

EVERY JAPANESE CANADIAN alive at the time can still remember that December 7th Sunday morning in 1941, when the radio announcer interrupted the usual programming to report the bone-chilling news that Japanese planes had bombed Pearl Harbour. Suddenly, the community's worst nightmare had become a reality.

At the age of ten Roy Inouye along with his mother and sisters, (one of whom is CBC vice-president, Margaret Lyons) packed their belongings into a couple of suitcases. Urged to take his most prized possession, the small boy selected a can of his favourite marbles. The family boarded a train in Mission, B.C., where Roy had been born, to embark on a trek that would take them halfway across the country. At North Bend, across from Boston Bar, the train made a short stop to take on fresh supplies of coal and water. Roy remembers being excited that his father, who had been sent to a nearby workcamp, was allowed to meet the train to say goodbye. Roy would not see his father again for six years.

On the train, whenever Roy began to sob his mother would repeat the Japanese equivalent of "boys do not cry." Yet throughout the four-day train trip from British Columbia to Winnipeg, whenever Roy woke during the night he heard the sound of weeping. He was surprised to discover that it was the men. In the secrecy of darkness they were releasing their pent-up fears about the future and their clenched rage at their inability to protect their families. As the train slowly made its way west, the coal-driven locomotive spewed volumes of black smoke that continually dusted the passengers with a fine black powder. At Rogers Pass in the Rocky Mountains they sat in pitch darkness as the train burrowed through an eight-mile tunnel of solid rock. As the train emerged into the bright sunlight, Roy was shocked by the eery sight. Save for the whites of their eyes, all the passengers were completely black, covered with soot. But the faces of the men showed tracks like little dry rivers, where their tears had flowed.

Roy recalls now that during his adolescence he always felt odd because he was the only one without a dad. When the family finally got together again after the war, the boy felt a stranger to his biological father. He would grow up to be a father himself, then a grandfather and a deeply religious Buddhist. As a member of the strategy and negotiation team of the NAJC, Roy Inouye would represent the view of the smaller Japanese Canadian communities.

By 1926 Shotaro (Tom) Shimizu was the successful owner of a hotel and restaurant on Prince Rupert's main street. That year he decided to return to his native prefecture in Japan to find a wife. With pride and some trepidation he brought back a nineteen-year-old bride, Kimiko, some fifteen years his junior. A pretty, educated, and high spirited woman, Kimiko had left her family and home in thriving commercial Osaka for a totally unknown future in a B.C. frontier port.

Now in her eighties, Kimiko Shimizu recalls with some bemusement her "disappointment" on discovering that Prince Rupert did not have a streetcar system and that her husband's hotel sported no chandeliers. A city girl, she was totally unprepared for the rigours of life in the Canadian bush. She personally knew no one who had emigrated and the only stories she knew of life in foreign lands were amusing accounts that she had read written by diplomats. Over the next fifteen years she bore four children and helped her husband through the difficult Depression years. By the time war was declared, the Shimizus had acquired and fully paid off an additional six properties.

In February 1942, after receiving the B.C. Security Commission's evacuation notice, Kimiko crammed six bags with toys, school books, bedding, and clothing. She was allowed one suitcase per person, so she even packed a small one for her youngest to carry. Like most Japanese Canadians, Tom and Kimiko Shimizu expected to return shortly, so they left their most valuable possessions securely locked in one room of their house. On March 23, 1942, while the family sadly walked away from their home down a snow-covered street, Kimiko fought back the desire to turn around, for one last look. She would never return to Prince Rupert.

At the Prince Rupert station, her eldest son Henry's grade seven teacher and classmates came by to see him off. When Kimiko saw her son talking dejectedly to his friends, tears welled up in her eyes. She saw him being being torn away from his friends and the life that he knew. After a stress-filled, anxiety-laden, three-day trip, the train came to a stop at its destination in Vancouver. Mysteriously, all the doors and windows were suddenly locked. Sealed inside their cars, unable to go to the toilet or move around within the train, the passengers felt tensions escalate as the temperature rose and the hours passed. Just as abruptly the car doors opened and the cool night air rushed in. In the twilight, six hundred Japanese Canadians from the north-coast settlements formed a line and silently walked towards the gate of the Hastings Park exhibition grounds. The group was herded towards some low buildings and Kimiko, clutching her youngest son's hand, was shown to a horse stall that would be home for her and her three youngest children for six months. Her husband and her oldest son, Henry, were taken away to be housed in a separate all-male dormitory building.

Six months later, in September 1942, the Shimizus boarded yet another train that took them to New Denver, an orchard town in the B.C. interior. Initially they lived in a tent while the cabin they would share with another family for the next four years was being completed. Kimiko remembers the intense cold in the winter as the green lumber of the new cabin dried and the icy winds blew through the chinks. She says the heat from the pot-bellied stove made the walls steam and the floors "were like a river" as the water came out of the wood.

In 1943, from their isolation in camps deep in the B.C. interior, Japanese Canadians, like Tom and Kimiko Shimizu, reacted in alarm at the news that the government was planning to liquidate all "enemy alien" property and possessions. By May 1943 they were shocked to learn that the hard-earned fruits of their labour had been sold by the Custodian of Enemy Property to the Veterans Land Act Board. The Shimizus joined a group of similarly dispossessed property owners from across the country who scraped together $6,500 for legal fees, and Tom Shimizu became one of the plaintiffs of a lawsuit against the Custodian. Each property owner was levied according to his resources, with Tom contributing $300 towards the cost of the claim. In 1947, years after the government had disposed of the properties and spent the proceeds, the Exchequer Court made public its ruling. Mr. Justice Joseph Thorson of the Exchequer Court, a member of the 1942 cabinet that had uprooted Japanese Canadians, issued a decision that effectively whitewashed the government's actions. By that time Tom, Kimiko, and their four children had moved yet again to Edmonton, where they both worked as hospital aides.

In a cruel sort of way, the treatment of Japanese Canadians during the 1940s should not have come as any great surprise. For Japanese Canadians the legal losses had really begun as early as 1903, when the English Privy Council upheld the 1895 B.C. Elections Act, which had legitimized our second-class status and reinforced all the other discriminatory laws that followed against Asians. Over the decades, statutes maintaining racial apartheid were customarily passed without discussion or debate. The decision taken in 1942 to imprison only Canada's Asian "enemy aliens" – and not the German and Italian communities – slipped by almost unnoticed.

Largely through the back room manoeuvring of the racist Vancouver politician Ian Mackenzie, who had vowed that as long as he was in public life there would be no Japanese in British Columbia, the provincial cabinet passed Order-in-Council P.C. 469 under the blanket powers of the War Measures Act.[2] Thereby the Custodian of Enemy Property was given the right to sell all the property in his care without the consent of the Japanese Canadian owners. At the time the sale of these assets was likened by critics in the Vancouver Consultative Committee, a small group of concerned white Canadians, to the Nazi Nuremburg laws that stripped Jews in Germany of their belongings.[3] This censure did not prevent the government from liquidating all the possessions of the interned community.

After the war, on July 18, 1947, following the U.S. precedent, the Canadian government established a Royal Commission to compensate Japanese Canadians for property losses suffered as a result of the Custodian's bargain basement prices. Three years later, British Columbia Justice Henry Irving Bird submitted his report and the federal government paid out $1,222,829 in damages – or approximately ten cents on the dollar – to the 1,434 Japanese Canadians who had made claims.

One such applicant was Torazo Iwasaki, who had owned 640 acres and 3,000 feet of shoreline on beautiful Salt Spring Island in the Strait of Georgia. The property had immense potential. While imprisoned in the Greenwood internment camp, Iwasaki had been informed that the Custodian had sold his property and that he would receive $4,932.99. Iwasaki refused to recognize the sale and claimed a further $66,000 from the Bird Inquiry. Bird upped Iwasaki's payment to $8,083, which Iwasaki reluctantly accepted after signing an official release.

During 1967, Canada's centennial year, Iwasaki, by this time eighty-seven years old, again challenged the Bird Commission's award and demanded a "voluntary" settlement of $1.5 million. The law suit alleged that given the price of land in the 1940s and the impropriety of the sale, such a figure was reasonable. The Custodian had sold the land to one of its own employees, Gavin Mouat, who at the time was a director of a large Vancouver Island real estate firm.[4] Not unexpectedly, three years later in 1970, the ninety-year-old Iwasaki lost in the Supreme Court of Canada, which upheld the ruling that the release Iwasaki had signed for the Bird Inquiry invalidated all further claims.[5]

In early 1942 the B.C. Security Commission planned to ship its "enemy alien" women, children, and elderly to camps in the interior and send able-bodied men off to work on road gangs in the east. The men, who would be separated by thousands of miles from their wives and children, feared for the safety of their families, given the abundance of racist toughs and the rigours of frontier life in the remote B.C. ghost towns. They also mistrusted the government's policy of breaking up families, which placed the heavy responsibilities of caring for the young and the elderly solely on the shoulders of the women.

Faced with this option, some Japanese Canadians decided to accept what seemed to be a more attractive offer from several provincial governments to keep families together. They chose to move directly from their homes on the west coast to sugar-beet farms in southern Alberta and Manitoba. When they arrived– packed into CP trains like so much human fodder – they were filled with shame when the local farmers converged to inspect them like slaves at an auction. The farmers wanted only healthy-looking families with lots of strong sons who could profitably perform the back-breaking labour of sugar-beet topping.

In Manitoba the Japanese Canadians had to once again begin the difficult task of re-establishing themselves and rebuilding their communities. They succeeded more rapidly than other displaced Japanese Canadians because the farming and fishing communities of the Fraser Valley and Steveston area were moved intact. Soon the prewar kinship networks and leadership structures that had been earlier transplanted from Japan to British Columbia once again put down roots in the less fertile soils of southern Manitoba. Respected and trusted prewar leaders such as Shinji Sato, an issei who had previously worked as an organizer for the New Westminster farmers' co-op, were instrumental in getting the Steveston fishers to move to Manitoba. A founding member of the Manitoba Japanese Canadian Community, a life-long trade unionist and a CCF member, Sato died in 1969 of a massive heart attack while delivering a speech at an aboriginal conference in Winnipeg.

Another important prewar leader was Harold Hirose, a nisei who had been the secretary-treasurer of the Surrey Berry Co-op Association. Harold Hirose arranged for two hundred Japanese Canadians from the Fraser Valley to work for the Manitoba Sugar Company on the understanding that their families would not be broken up. Immediately upon reaching Manitoba, Sato, Hirose, and a handful of others, appalled at the sharecropper working and living conditions, clandestinely organized the Japanese sugar-beet workers into a union. Threatening an illegal strike, they managed to negotiate better wages and living arrangements from the federal Department of Labour.

Those first years of resettlement in Manitoba were hard. Initially

Japanese Canadians were banned from living in Winnipeg and prohibited by law from purchasing property. Landlords slammed doors in their faces and only the most difficult, menial, and poorly paid jobs in the foundries and tanneries were available to them. Early in life their children had to learn to fight with their fists or to run from their tormentors. At the beginning only the Jews and the Mennonites were willing to hire these slant-eyed Canadians.

On the farms many were unable to earn enough money to support themselves, even with the combined labour of their children. Families were housed in windy shacks, little better than chicken coops, in the middle of barren farm fields. In the winter they would wake up in the morning with their hair frozen to the walls. Without telephones or cars and confined by curfew regulations and travel restrictions, emergency visits to doctors were impossible. Many a frantic mother sat by anxiously at night unable to seek help while her child vomited up blood.

In 1942, the Hiroses became the first Japanese Canadians allowed to live in Winnipeg. They helped other families find jobs and shelter as gradually more and more Japanese Canadians left the sugar-beet farms and began to trickle into Winnipeg. In the city, even with his accountancy training Harold Hirose was only able to find work in a Jewish seniors' home as a waiter and dishwasher. His wife Florence was hired to make beds. He was denied work as a taxi driver or in an accounting firm because those jobs required contact with the public. Harold recalls now that often when he and his wife returned home late at night from work, a tearful and desperate Japanese Canadian family would be waiting for them in the dark hallway outside their rented rooms.

In 1945, after years of having his application rejected by the Canadian army, Harold was finally accepted into the British and then the Canadian army. By his own estimate, the oldest Japanese Canadian recruit, he saw action in Malaysia and India. One day, remarking on Harold's uniform, a white Canadian soldier asked Harold what would happen if he were captured by the Japanese. Harold answered philosophically, "The Japanese will cut off my head first, and then they'll cut off yours."

In June 1946, when Harold was discharged from the Canadian army, he discovered that nothing had changed. Back in Canada, he was still an enemy alien. He was unable to return to the west coast of British Columbia. His father's fifteen-acre farm in Surrey, B.C., had been purchased by the Veterans Land Act Board in 1943 and was distributed to returning white Canadian soldiers after the war. Although he was a veteran, Harold was denied the franchise and the rights of Canadian citizenship. To this day, Harold Hirose still retains his optimism and belief in Canada. He is a mainstay of the Winnipeg and Manitoba Japanese Canadian community, and during the redress years, Harold was the NAJC's treasurer and a respected adviser to President Art Miki and the strategy/negotiation team.

During the war the only organized resistance to the Canadian government's internment orders came from the Nisei Mass Evacuation Group (NMEG). At the time, these Canadian born nisei were youngsters. They formed NMEG to organize opposition to the government's persecution of Japanese Canadians. In April 1942, NMEG's leaders were clandestinely addressing gatherings of nisei up and down the B.C. coast. Later that month, acting on a tip, the RCMP raided a NMEG executive meeting being held at the Patricia Hotel on the fringes of Vancouver's Japantown. Two of NMEG's organizers, Fujikazu Tanaka and Yukio Shimoda, were picked up, held in Vancouver's immigration centre, and then shipped thousands of miles away to a prisoner of war camp outside Port Arthur-Fort William (now Thunder Bay) in Angler, Ontario. Angler, unlike the internment camps in the B.C. interior, housed Japanese Canadian "troublemakers" and German POWs behind barbed wire and within the sights of rifles. NMEG's vice-president, Shig Uchibori, narrowly escaped RCMP arrest only because he arrived late at the Patricia Hotel meeting. Seeing uniformed mounties at the windows, he turned and went underground. Over the summer of 1942 other NMEG members were picked up and detained. Most of them were held for at least a year in Angler.

On NMEG's behalf, while in hiding, Uchibori continued to negotiate with the B.C. Security Commission. On May 19, 1942, NMEG issued a manifesto calling on the Canadian government to release from a POW camp in Petawawa, Ontario, the Japanese Canadians who had been arrested for resisting their relocation to road camps; to cease the policy of breaking up families; and to provide land, housing, hospitals, schools, clothing, and food for the Japanese Canadians being resettled in the B.C. interior. By the end of June 1942, the Commission had agreed to intern families as units and to send the Petawawa prisoners to the Angler POW prison. Two NMEG leaders, Shimoda and Kanbara resolved to remain in Angler until the camp was closed in 1946 because, as Tameo Kanbara put it years later, "We felt responsible for having organized NMEG and believed that we should show our *ganbari* (resistance) to the government until the end." Kanbara's son Bryce, a well-known Hamilton artist and community organizer, was a member of the NAJC's strategy/negotiation team.

Another nisei who joined NMEG in 1942 was Torontonian Harry Yonekura. A teenager at the time, Harry recalls attending a large NMEG meeting of nisei fishers in Steveston. At the conclusion of the emotional meeting, NMEG organizer Fuji Tanaka urged those present to show their opposition to the Canadian government's actions by tearing up their enemy-alien ID papers. There was hushed silence as the men contemplated this act of defiance. Suddenly the room was filled with the sound of two hundred papers being shredded and thrown to the ground.

Today, sixty-nine year old Harry Yonekura still recalls his anger at the government's policy of sending the men to road camps and the women and children to deserted ghost towns. He remembers seeing a Japanese Canadian woman grovelling on her knees at the feet of an RCMP officer, tearfully begging him not to send her husband away. When he saw that, Harry says, "Something in me broke. I knew that it was wrong." The memory made him tear up his ID at the Steveson meeting. But he was filled with fear just the same: any Japanese Canadian without identification papers could be immediately imprisoned. Up to that time Japanese Canadians had co-operated with the B.C. Security Commission. After that first act of rebellion, no one could predict how the Commission would react. Indeed, several months after the meeting Harry was picked up on the streets of Vancouver and thrown in jail. Like the other members of NMEG he was sent to Angler where he was imprisoned for eleven months. In all, about seven hundred Japanese Canadians were held in Angler. The experience served to make Harry Yonekura a Toronto community activist and firm supporter of redress.

Retired journalist Frank Moritsugu was a nineteen-year-old teenager when he heard the news that the Japanese imperial army had bombed Pearl Harbor. Frank recalls running home after hearing the radio broadcast, terrified at what had happened. Prophetically he realized that the secure little Japanese Canadian world he knew in Vancouver had collapsed and that "nothing could ever be the same again." Several months later his father, a gardener and Japanese national, was put aboard a train filled with other issei bound for a construction camp in Yellowhead, B.C.

In April 1942 Frank, a Canadian-born Japanese male of military age, was sent by the government to a road camp in Yard Creek, near Revelstoke in the mountains of eastern British Columbia. Not long afterwards Frank's brother Ken turned eighteen and was also dispatched to the camp. Under the watchful eyes of armed sentries from the Veteran's Guard, the two brothers spent seventeen months clearing bush and blasting rock for the Trans-Canada Highway. By the fall of 1942, his mother and younger brothers and sisters had been sent to the Tashme internment camp, near Hope, B.C.

Frank's parents, realizing that they'd have a better chance of keeping the family together and seeing to their children's education if they left Tashme, volunteered to move to labour-starved eastern Canada. The B.C. Security Commission assigned the Moritsugus to work on the farm of the Ontario premier, Mitchell Hepburn, near St. Thomas, Ontario. In 1944 Frank was permitted to join them to work as a farm hand. When an army recruiting team visited the Hepburn farm a year later, Frank decided to enlist. He recalls arguing for two days and nights with his parents, who asked him how he could think of fighting for Canada after the way the community had been treated. In the end, like the issei who had fought for Canada in the First World War, Frank joined up to gain rights at home.

Although many nisei had tried to sign up throughout the Second World War, they had been turned down. But by late 1944 the British were desperate for interpreters who could read and speak Japanese, to help translate captured enemy documents and interrogate Japanese POWs in the Southeast Asian theatre. The British command convinced the Canadian military to allow Canadian nisei into the allied forces to perform these important duties. Like Frank Moritsugu, many of these nisei recruits joined the Special Force 136, which was sent to assist in the Allied takeovers of Saigon, Singapore, and Jakarta.

Throughout the war years a debate had raged in the B.C. cabinet as to what should be the ultimate fate of these "yellow aliens." Ian Mackenzie and other racist B.C. politicians lobbied to have the entire community freighted to Japan. Members of the Co-operative Committee on Japanese Canadians (CCJC) condemned mass deportations as fascist. The CCJC urged the government to disperse the 22,000 across the country so the Japanese Canadians would be assimilated and disappear.[6]

Four months after the war had ended, on Saturday December 15, 1945, the federal government passed Order-in-Council P.C. 7355 authorizing the deportation to starving Japan of almost half of the community.[7] Japanese Canadian families isolated for years in the B.C. interior were emotionally and physically torn apart as they agonized over the alternatives posed by the Canadian government: either repatriate to Japan or relocate yet again, to eastern Canada. Those who chose Japan did so out of desperation. One internee of the Angler prisoner of war camp, in an intercepted letter to his sister, wrote that he was going to Japan because "The white people hate us and we have no other place to go."[8]

Both choices posed fearful unknowns. Japan was a defeated, war-devastated nation, but for the older issei it offered at least the assurance of the familiar and the support of relatives. They also realized that another resettlement in Canada would be financially and emotionally difficult for the elderly and for families with young children. At night in the camps rumours passed from shack to shack conveying the fear that racism in eastern Canada might be even worse than in British Columbia.

In turn the Co-operative Committee (CCJC) organized a national network that included groups such as the Young Women's Christian Association, civil libertarians, and the churches. With the ending of the war – and for almost the first time since they had come to this country – Japanese Canadians found that they were not alone. The CCJC established a chapter in Toronto to fight the deportations. The CCJC's lawyer Andrew Brewin filed a declaratory motion questioning the legal validity of the deportation of Canadian citizens and residents. The writs were issued in the names of Yukata Shimoyama, a Canadian-born Japanese mushroom farm labourer living in Port Credit, Ontario, and Yae Nasu, a Toronto issei widow, the wife of a naturalized citizen and the mother of seven Canadian-born children.[9] The issues, ultimately argued before the Privy Council in England, were that the orders to expel persons of the Japanese race were too vague as they applied to Canadians and that the federal government did not have the power to deport and exile its own citizens.

Given a court record that upheld disenfranchisement, legal discrimination, and theft of property, the Privy Council decision should have come as no surprise. On December 2, 1946, the English Court ruled against the Japanese Canadians and decreed that the Canadian government could do whatever it wanted, pursuant to the powers of the War Measures Act. [10] While the court deliberated, some four thousand people left Canada on five ships for Japan. In the end about twenty per cent of the Japanese Canadian community were sent to Japan, a country many of them had never known. Half were Canadian-born children under the age of sixteen. [11] For at least one family, repatriation to Japan was a death sentence. A destitute sixty-six-year-old father of seven children, whose Fraser Valley farm had been sold by the Custodian, returned with his wife and family to his ancestral farm outside of Hiroshima. Most of the family's original land had long since been sold off, and with no legal claim to the remainder the elderly parents were forced to work in the coal mines and within months they died of malnutrition. [12]

Almost every family in Canada was broken up as some moved east and others boarded ships bound for Japan. My father's eldest brother, Rinzo, took his wife and four unwilling Canadian-born children back to the family home in Shiga-ken. One of my cousins recalls his stark memories of Japan – the house totally destroyed, the pain of hunger, and the feelings of alienation. All of the children immediately set about working to return home to British Columbia.

There was a difference in the experience of the issei – who had been born in Japan and were being repatriated – and the "exiles" – the nisei, born in Canada who were being sent off to a foreign country (Japan). Many of the exiles were like Canadian-born George Tsuruda, who opposed his parents' resolution to return to Japan after the war's end. In fact, as soon the U.S. troop carrier *General Meigs* moored in the port of Yokohama and unloaded its human cargo, which included the Tsuruda family and five hundred other Japanese Canadians, sixteen-year-old George tried to stow away and return to Canada.

Weeks earlier, before boarding the ship in Vancouver and just after he had completed grade nine at New Denver High School, George was required to renounce his Canadian citizenship. He remembers secretly crossing his fingers and crying as he wrote his name backwards, hoping that somehow he wouldn't be held accountable for his actions. Like the child he was, George wished that the grim reality he faced would magically transform itself and that life would revert to the days when he wasn't an enemy alien.

Under the circumstances, his parents' choice was a rational one. George's father was physically crippled and weak from a serious stroke he had suffered in the internment camps, and he was worried about how he could support his six dependent children in Canada. George's mother believed the family would be warmly received by her kin in Japan and that they could all live on her parents' farm in Kyushu. Instead, they found a Japan that had been levelled by bombs. It was too much to hope that their relatives would welcome additional mouths to share the handfuls of bug-infested grains boiled into the mealy gruel that was their daily rations.

In Japan, faced with near starvation and virtual homelessness, George – like many other teenage Japanese Canadians – chose to work for the U.S. armed forces as an interpreter. In the army camps at least people spoke English and life was familiarly North American. Unlike the rest of the hungry and destitute Japanese population, Frank had a roof over his head, three meals a day, and a small monthly stipend that he carefully sent home to help feed his family. Without proper citizenship and a nation he could call home, George felt utterly hopeless and full of despair. Now, remembering those dark years, he says that a man without a country has to be the loneliest person in the world. In 1949, as soon as the Canadian government established an embassy in Japan, George applied for and ecstatically received a Canadian passport. A year later he returned to Canada. The American GIs he had worked with during the previous three years all chipped in two months' salary to buy him a suitcase full of clothes and his passage across the Pacific. Ironically, these U.S. occupation soldiers had recognized that George Tsuruda was a Canadian and not Japanese, and they paid for him to go home.

Back in Canada, George spent a year working with a CPR labour gang laying track in northern British Columbia, where he earned enough money to send to his destitute family and to his American benefactors. George exchanged letters with his GI buddies until the outbreak of the Korean war, when they were sent to the battle front and he lost touch with them. The next year, after his father died in Japan, George as the oldest child and sole breadwinner had to abandon plans of returning to school. Over the following years he brought his two younger brothers back to Canada and continued to send all his paycheques to Japan to support his widowed mother and siblings. He did this until all the children finished their education. In the meantime George had joined the Canadian armed forces and managed through correspondence courses to get his high-school graduation diploma and learn a trade. In all he spent thirty-two years in the Canadian service. Today, married with three children of his own, George remembers only too well the painful years and difficult hardships of his younger life.

In 1942 in the United States, Fred Korematsu, Min Yasui, and Gordon Hirabayashi decided to defy the American wartime restrictions against American Japanese. The men were picked up, charged, tried, and found guilty of various curfew and exclusion violations. Each young American was sentenced to imprisonment.

Four decades later, with the assistance of a group of sansei Bay area lawyers, these men, now retired grandfathers, decided to appeal their convictions as being unconstitutional. After fighting legal battles all the way up to the U.S. Supreme Court, Korematsu, Yasui, and Hirabayashi were eventually successful in having their findings of guilt "vacated." The Court decided that during their original trials, government lawyers had incorrectly suppressed evidence. In the words of Judge Patel, speaking about the Korematsu conviction, the Roosevelt administration had relied on unsubstantiated charges, and on the racist views of General John De Witt to justify Japanese American internment. [13] De Witt is famous for his remark, "Once a Jap, always a Jap" as the explanation for the state's actions.

An American by birth, a Canadian through choice, and a Japanese by ancestry, seventy-three-year-old Gordon Hirabayashi has played a unique role in both the U.S. and Canadian redress movements. Now a retired university professor living in Edmonton, Gordon has been a practising Quaker since his college days. A man of strong conviction and courage, Gordon is an American civil rights hero. In 1942 American Japanese, like Japanese Canadians, were being rounded up and shipped to isolated and barren locations away from the west coast. At the age of twenty-four, in his last year at the University of Seattle, Gordon decided he would refuse executive order 9066 because of his religious convictions and his belief that the order was unconstitutional and discriminatory. He telephoned his parents to inform them of his fateful decision. The Hirabayashis, non-denominational pacifist Christians whose lives mirrored their religious practices, understood his actions. Still, his mother asked Gordon to accompany them and to protest the government's actions from Tule Lake internment camp, where the family was to be sent. As he hung up the phone, Gordon, as eldest son, felt guilty for abandoning his parents and refusing to comply with his mother's wishes. In May 1942, escorted by his Quaker lawyer Arthur Barnett, Gordon turned himself in to the Seattle officials. Immediately he was imprisoned in the federal holding tank that occupied the top floors of the King County jail in downtown Seattle.

One evening months later Gordon was awakened in his cell by a guard escorting a tiny captive. The official demanded, "What should I do with this guy?" Gordon peered through the gloom and immediately recognized his father. Surprised, he asked his dad, "What are you doing here?" Mr. Hirabayashi senior replied, "Both your mother and I have been brought to jail to testify at your trial." The charge against Gordon was simply that he was of Japanese ancestry. Accordingly, the state had subpoenaed his parents to prove its case.

Gordon's mother, an issei farmer's wife, had never been inside a jail before. Fearful, she had formed her image of *hakujin* prisons from the book, *The Count of Monte Cristo*. In Tule Lake internment camp she had conjured up visions of her son being chained to the walls of a dungeon, tortured by sadistic guards. Frightened upon finding herself brought to the King County jail women's section, her eyes lit upon the only familiar object that she knew, a broken-down piano. To give herself comfort she quietly began to play familiar hymns. As she looked up, she found herself encircled by women, who began to accompany her in song, with tears welling up in their eyes. Surrounded by prostitutes and petty thieves, Mrs. Hirabayashi was asked, "What are you doing in the slammer?" She explained in broken English about the unusual circumstance whereby as federal witnesses she and her husband were being held in jail to testify at her son's trial.

Early in the morning of his district court trial, Gordon and his father waited for his mother to come downstairs to accompany them to the courthouse. When she did appear, they were shocked. For the first time in her life, she had had her hair set, her face made up, and her nails manicured by the other women prisoners. Later she told Gordon that she did not know why the women were being held, but she had found them to be a sympathetic and friendly group of people.

At the conclusion of his hearing, Gordon was found guilty of curfew and exclusion violations and sentenced to ninety days. Instantly an appeal was launched, questioning the constitutional validity of the wartime racist laws. Recognizing the legal significance of the challenges, the U.S. Supreme Court decided to hear the appeal. Awaiting the date of his second trial, Gordon, a popular inmate, was dubbed "mayor" of the federal holding tank by both his jailers and the other convicts. Unlike most prisoners who were there for only a few days, Gordon knew his way around, having already spent five months in jail.

A week after the court's decision, his parents were taken back to the Tule Lake internment camp by a federal marshall. On parting, Mr. Hirabayashi told Gordon that he was no longer worried about his son's safety because he had witnessed how everyone in the holding cell called him "mayor."

One morning while preparing for his Supreme Court appeal, Gordon received a letter from his mother, who described a recent visit that she had had from two American Japanese issei mothers. On behalf of all American Japanese, these white-haired women had bowed deeply and thanked her for her son's courageous stand. Gordon recalls that for the first time in months he felt a large weight of guilt lifted from his shoulders. Now with the approval of his mother, he said he felt free, in spite of being locked up behind iron bars.

Finally, in October 1942, the date Gordon had been waiting for arrived: his hearing before the Supreme Court of the United States. Throughout his captivity Gordon had always believed that the American

Constitution would protect all its citizens, including American Japanese. But, at the conclusion of an all- day hearing, the Supreme Court bench upheld the earlier decision and found Gordon guilty of curfew violations. The Supreme Court chose to ignore the more difficult constitutional question of whether U.S. citizens could be restricted in their movements solely on the basis of race. Disappointed, Gordon returned to jail. Shortly thereafter, he was sent to Spokane to complete his sentence. Forty years later, still an idealist, Gordon played an important role in both the U.S. and Canadian redress movements.

The Canadian redress movement may have started in July 1946, when 128 Japanese Canadian internees from the Angler POW camp refused to accept either of the government's two options: relocation east or repatriation to Japan. In the face of the bizarre insurrection at Angler, and uncertain about what action to take, the federal government shipped the lot of them one thousand miles west to a former Royal Canadian Air Force depot four miles south of Moose Jaw, Saskatchewan, where a temporary "hostel" had been set up.

By late 1946 there were some 280 people in the camp. The internees were offered employment, mostly on sugar-beet or wheat farms, but many of them were not willing or able to take on this kind of work. They wanted instead to be allowed to go back to their homes, to be treated like any other Canadian citizens. They wanted to be compensated for their seized businesses and homes and for their five years in internment camps. Tsuneo Naka, one of these *ganbari* or resisters, said on a Moose Jaw radio program in 1948, "The government took us out of our homes, interned us as enemy aliens, and seized our property, all without cause. It may have been legal, but it wasn't justice – and it is justice we want."[14]

By May 30, 1948, the government, trying to clear out the hostel, presented the internees with a notice to vacate. Eventually most of the residents reluctantly drifted away, leaving behind some eleven "diehard" internees, their families and twenty-four single male internees. In August, in a last effort to close down the camp, the government announced the termination of all food supplies.

One of the internees at both Angler and Moose Jaw was Tsuneo Naka's fifty-nine-year-old issei father, Tomijiro Naka, who told his story to *The New Canadian* in 1947. Tomijiro Naka had owned a small business in Vancouver, a store that had just finally managed to turn a profit before the war. To keep the store afloat Naka had worked in a sawmill while his wife ran the business, and he'd poured all of his life savings into it. In 1942 the Custodian of Enemy Property came and took the store away. Naka, refusing to go to work in the Rockies where he'd be separated from his family, ended up being taken into custody by the RCMP and "shoved into a concentration camp" in Angler.

From the Moose Jaw camp, Naka said, "We are called 'diehard ex-internees' but that is not true. I have every intention of moving out of here. I don't want to stay here and I would like to go out and start life again just like every other evacuee has done." Naka asked, "Who is responsible for us? Who was responsible for the misery I went through behind barbed wire for four years? What did I do to deserve all this punishment? The sooner the government gives me a satisfactory deal, the sooner I will get out of this place. My store has been sold without my consent. My life savings are gone. Is this democracy?"[15]

One of the leaders of the *ganbari* was Hirokichi Isomura, a World War I Canadian war veteran who had been wounded at Vimy Ridge and later, in 1931, became one of the few Japanese Canadians granted the franchise. In a book published in Japan in 1935 another Japanese Canadian war veteran, Sachimaro Moro-oka, described a revealing WWI incident involving Isomura. According to Moro-oka, Isomura once came upon a German soldier who was obviously near death. The German asked for some water and Isomura gave him a drink from his canteen. A Canadian solider came along, pushed Isomura aside, and stabbed the German with his bayonet. Isomura, furious at this needless cruelty, yelled at the Canadian, saying the German was going to die anyway. The two of them began to go at each other with their bayonets, but they were separated before any further damage could be done.[16]

At the Moose Jaw hostel, enraged at the Canadian government's treatment of veterans like himself who had proved their loyalty to Canada in a previous war, Isomura led a sit-down strike in the corridor outside the office of the camp's supervisor. The strikers demanded the lifting of the travel restrictions preventing Japanese Canadians from returning to British Columbia's west coast. After three fruitless weeks the protestors gave up and returned to their barracks.

The impasse at the camp dragged on and by mid-1948, three years after the war, the Canadian government was becoming more and more embarrassed by the presence of these internees. On July 15, 1948, exasperated at their demands for redress and their refusal to be relocated, the government sent in twelve men who packed up the residents' belongings into a few vans and unceremoniously deposited the goods in an empty field north of the barracks. The local sheriff gave the Japanese Canadians thirty minutes to leave the hostel. The last two holdouts were Tomijiro Naka, the issei shop owner, and Suekichi Miyagawa. After being dragged from the barracks they pitched a pup tent outside the hostel for a further 136 days, until they finally accepted an offer from the federal Department of Labour to go live in an "old folks home" in New Denver, B.C.

The story of the Moose Jaw internees fell off the pages of Adachi's book, *The Enemy That Never Was*, in a jumble of words and fast cut images. Adachi himself seemed unable to completely unravel the story or decipher the motives of the men. He asked: "Were these people, then, martyrs, heroes or simply fanatics? They were the only people throughout the entire period to carry resistance or *ganbari* to such desperate lengths." [17]

When I was in my twenties and desperate to find Japanese Canadian role models, I wanted to believe that these refuseniks were indeed heroes and that some of their fire flowed in my own veins. Yet there was a distinct element of tragedy in their story. As Adachi concluded, "The revolt of the Moose Jaw hostellers was a lonely, hopeless act, sustained against the odds, thoroughly against the grain of the more conformist and reticent behaviour generally typical of the evacuees." [18]

There was even a rumour that this small band of desperados had resisted the Canadian government out of support for the Japanese Imperial army. [19]

Years later, in my speeches and writings on redress, I would routinely mention the Moose Jaw incident, hoping that someone would come forward and mention that they had been there. But no one ever did. Then a friend, Japanese Canadian filmmaker, Jesse Nishihata, gave me a lead. The Naka family had relocated to Estevan, Saskatchewan. A long-distance operator gave me the phone number of one "A. Naka." When a flat Canadian voice answered I wondered, could this very ordinary-sounding person be one of those cowboy desperados? How could this man, who sounded like my uncle, be that firebrand Tsuneo Naka who had once proclaimed on Moose Jaw radio for all to hear that he was fighting for redress? On the phone Tony Naka told me that all his father wanted was to be treated like a British subject, according to "British justice." He said that after his interview on CHAB radio in 1948, the Japanese Canadian *ganbari* were flooded with food and blankets from white Moose Jaw locals. However, shortly after being kicked out of the Moose Jaw barracks, Tony had been advised by a Winnipeg lawyer, Saul Cherniak, to forget the whole thing, as if that were possible.

Now, over forty years later, Tony and his family in Estevan, Saskatchewan are uncomfortable speaking of the past. Martyrs, heroes, or fanatics? In their day they made their statement and tenaciously dug in. They were waiting for justice. Like the Moose Jaw *ganbari* in their long holdout, the Japanese Canadian community also patiently marked time. On the surface, the few unremarkable green shoots gave little indication of the depth of resentment, anger, or pain that lay beneath the passive exterior. Yet during the forty years of waiting, just below the surface, the seeds of injustice had put down a full network of deep roots.

Five hundred Japanese Canadians demonstrated in Ottawa in April 1988 for the Redress settlement.

5 | The Tide Turns: Inside the Japanese Canadian Community

Perhaps we want nothing better
than to forget the raw wounds of yesterday,
to cover the scar with delusions of security,
but what was once taken away
can be taken away again.
Who knows but that the next time
will be made easier for the plunderers
because we shrugged and said "Shikataga-nai"
(it can't be helped)

– Muriel Kitagawa, 1946[1]

BEGINNING IN 1946, Canada's eighteen thousand tired enemy aliens gathered up their personal possessions and children and prepared once again to relocate to an unknown destination. These Canadians who chose to stay in Canada had voted with their feet. A further 4,319 disspirited Japanese Canadians gathered at the immigration shed on Vancouver's waterfront and boarded ships like the S.S. *Marine Angel* and the S.S. *Marine Falcon* bound for Japan.

It wasn't until 1947 that the POW camps would be completely emptied, and it would be another two years before the Canadian government would permit Japanese Canadians to return to within one hundred miles of Canada's Pacific Ocean. By that time they had no homes, businesses, or communities to return to. Ian Mackenzie's dream of wiping away all traces of the Japanese Canadian presence in British Columbia had been realized. The property of an entire minority had been impounded and sold without their consent. To add insult to injury, the costs of their imprisonment were deducted from the profits of the sales. Unlike prisoners of war, enemy nationals under the Geneva Convention, or American Japanese, Canadians of Japanese ancestry were forced to pay for their own internment.

Understandably, the community had divided loyalties. When an issei was asked how he felt about the war between Japan and Canada, his response was: when your mother and father are fighting, how can you support one side or the other, or say that there is a winner? Doubtless considered traitors by some of their family members back in Japan for remaining in their adoptive country, the Canadian issei nonetheless felt deep ties to the country of their birth. They would take these feelings of love to their graves. How could it be otherwise? The issei were raised on the myth of Yamato and the uniqueness of the Japanese people. As a third-generation Canadian of Japanese ancestry, I also have my heart-strings tugged puppet-like by a people I do not know and with whom I share little.

Today, in a country filled with immigrants, refugees, and exiles, it is acceptable to search for your roots and to acknowledge these dual loyalties. But for most of Canada's history, for those of us from non-Anglo-Saxon heritages, the cost exacted for Canadian citizenship was slash and burn surgery and unconditional submersion. For my generation, assimilation demanded a denial of our ethnicity. Yet the aching pain remained. Uncomfortable within our own skins, we secretly tried to reconcile our reflections in the mirror with the reality that lay just beyond the front door. Even with today's official policy of multiculturalism, we minorities know that in the end we must finally cut the octopus-like tenacles that bind us to virtually every nation on the globe.

Our parents, the nisei, were willing to pay this price, and they strove ever harder to become a hundred and fifty per cent Canadian. They hoped in so doing to gain acceptance, to win the franchise, and to finally receive equal citizenship rights with whites. Of all our generations in Canada, the nisei had best learned the lesson of the bamboo. Yet, even knowing the nisei's deeply held convictions of honour, family, and duty, as a young girl I saw their refusal to fight for what was theirs as being distinctly un-North American. John Wayne might be slow-witted, I thought as I watched the Saturday matinee westerns, but when he was backed into a corner he was prepared to shoot it out.

I was not alone in misunderstanding my parents' generation. Growing up as adolescents in British Columbia, the nisei were also ashamed of their immigrant parents' weird ways, their pigeon English, and mongolian, heavily lidded eyes. Yet even dressed in Canadian clothes and with their perfect hip talk, the nisei were nonetheless told by white adolescent ushers to sit in the Oriental sections of the Vancouver movie theatres. They were cut to the quick by the sharp knives of racism. Today, all bear flesh wounds where their yellow skin was slit by the cold steel.

As the years passed, the Japanese Canadian survivors of the camps tried to put the past behind them and slowly bury the trauma of the war years under successive layers of scar tissue. Still, at night around kitchen tables, angry voices debated the community's future. In the middle of the war, in 1943, a group of Toronto nisei, founded the Japanese Canadian Committee for Democracy.[2] Still barely alive was the issei dream of equality. After the war, in 1947, this Committee was converted into the community's first national organization, the National Japanese Canadian Citizens' Association (NJCCA), with chapters in Quebec, Ontario, Manitoba, Alberta, and British Columbia. The NJCCA was formed by idealistic nisei in search of what seemed, at the time, to be as elusive as the holy grail: the end of racial persecution. Roger Obata was elected their first president. Tom Shoyama, an admired nisei leader, reported that in 1947-48 the NJCCA had a "very brief discussion about the possibility of seeking redress." The idea, he says, was quickly dismissed "as being so remote as not to be worth fighting for."[3]

For two decades following the war, Japanese Canadians were completely self-absorbed. The NJCCA had become more or less irrelevant, largely relegated to organizing summer picnics and Christmas bazaars. It had abandoned its critical edge. Instead the NJCCA's apolitical mask covered a shattered community's face distorted by phobias and real fears. For the most part the NJCCA epitomized the nisei's public persona. Afraid of backlash, frightened to criticize authority, avoidant of real democracy, the NJCCA simply reflected the ever-present community nightmare of a resurgence of racism.

The idea of redress was not to resurface for almost thirty years, occasioned in 1977 by the community's celebration of our first hundred years in this country. In our remembrance, the sweet memories were darkened by long shadows. The speeches were laced with coded references to pain and anger. For the first time curious sansei demanded an explanation. The sansei, holding the issei's soft hands or looking deep into the nisei's avoiding eyes, could sense that lying just below the surface was a bitter truth. A committee to consider appropriate forms of redress was formed.

A gentle breeze of change was in the air. In 1980, in a re-structuring that saw two new centres added, the NJCCA renamed itself the National Association of Japanese Canadians (NAJC). That year, at the NAJC's first national convention in Vancouver, the first of many I would attend, representatives from fifteen centres elected a new president, nisei Gordon Kadota, a member of a respected Vancouver family and a successful businessman. Kadota, fluently bilingual (in Japanese and English), was able to bridge the language gap with the issei, something none of the sansei leadership was later able to do.

Still, the community's political old guard continued to be represented by men such as George Imai, a nisei Toronto school teacher with close ties to the Liberal Party. Imai had been the president of the old NJCCA in the late 1970s and had become the acting head of the Redress Committee. He was accustomed to speaking with impunity for all Japanese Canadians. To this day Imai still commands a certain loyalty, perhaps because to those in the community who refused to speak up for their rights he represents the old values of *shikataga-nai* (resignation) and *enryo* (restraint).

Under Kadota's leadership, Japanese Canadian community representatives on the NAJC National Council began the long and difficult process of trying to wrest George Imai from his position as the association's public spokesman and to develop a truly representative position on what many in the community had wanted to keep secret and forgotten.[4] In 1981 in Vancouver a group of sansei formed the Japanese Canadian Centennial Project (JCCP) to push for a public examination of the government's wartime treatment of its yellow enemy aliens. In 1983 the ante was raised outside the community when NAJC President Kadota appeared before a House of Commons Special Joint Committee on the Constitution. In his opening volley Kadota declared, "Our history in Canada is a legacy of racism made legitimate by our political institutions."[5]

Meanwhile, adding fuel to the fire, Imai continued to act autocratically in what he thought was the community's best interests. Indeed, without the knowledge or authorization of the NAJC Imai had for years been holding behind-the-scenes discussions with government politicians such as Toronto M.P. David Collenette, the Liberal Minister of Multiculturalism under Trudeau. Press accounts quoted Collonette as saying that the cabinet would be presented with a redress settlement that consisted of an "acknowledgement of injustices" tied to a $5 million fund, which would benefit not only Japanese Canadians "but all Canadians." Alarmed by the press reports, some of us in Toronto and the JCCP of Vancouver began organizing community symposiums and letter-writing campaigns.

Redress was assuming a national profile. On June 27, 1983, Liberal Minister of Justice Mark MacGuigan, replying to questions in the House of Commons from M.P. Lynn McDonald, said, "The matter is indeed under some consideration by Government. It is far from being ripe at the present time." For the following months, there were occasional press references to what *Toronto Star* columnist Joe Serge called "Canada's shame."

By 1984 editorials across the country had begun to take up the issue and to advise the Trudeau government that "Japanese-Canadians have waited long enough for compensation; they should have to wait no longer." On the quantum question, however, there wasn't editorial unanimity. Some, like the *Montreal Gazette*, advised that "Japanese-Canadians should seek collective, rather than individual compensation. Otherwise some claimants may die before their claim is honoured."[6] Others, like *The Toronto Sun*, criticized Trudeau for being a "statist" and described the wartime property confiscations as "outright theft." The *Sun* argued that a "cash payment to an individual does not give the state more power ... the Japanese are self-reliant individuals. Cash payments to them would end the problem. And giving them money would also set a precedent that Trudeau might be particularly afraid of: Namely that the expropriation of land by the state is wrongful and requires compensation."[7] However, *The Globe and Mail*, while criticizing Trudeau for his refusal to compensate, remained neutral on "whatever form the compensation takes."[8]

Within the Liberal party there was also a difference of opinion. In his maiden speech in the Senate, Liberal Jerry Grafstein chose to speak on the issue of Japanese Canadian redress. Senator Grafstein introduced a motion that the government apologize to Japanese Canadians for their incarceration and property confiscations and that a Commissioner be appointed to "adjudicate partial compensation for losses" up to a maximum of $50 million. Grafstein concluded that support for his motion would "give a new definition to Canadian justice."[9]

Anxious that the Liberals might act unilaterally before calling the 1984 federal election, the NAJC held press conferences around the country condemning the government's high-handedness. On June 20, 1984, I read a prepared statement to the press on behalf of President Art Miki at a meeting at Toronto's Holy Trinity Church, rejecting Collonette's offer of a "trust fund to promote racial harmony." Well-known members of our community, including columnist Ken Adachi, author Joy Kogawa, professor Tom Shoyama, and broadcaster David Suzuki, issued a press release on June 18, 1984, criticizing Collenette's offer as "very unilateral and undemocratic" and urging the Liberals to negotiate with the community's elected representatives, the NAJC.

The ensuing public debate appeared to confirm the astonishing news that the federal government was unilaterally planning to apologize to Japanese Canadians. The community was taken by surprise. As in our past, unexpected actions from Ottawa were forcing this unwilling Canadian minority to rouse itself from its depressed slumber and sit up and take notice. The dry mouths of Japanese Canadians were filled with a sour mixture of fear and outrage: fear because all still carried wounds of the war; outrage because the community had not been consulted and the sum of money being mentioned as a settlement was so paltry as to be an insult. But our feelings of anger were continually in danger of being drowned by feelings of dread. Although the redress movement of the 1980s was ignited and fuelled by rage, before the flickering embers could develop into a community movement the mass apprehensions of *shikataga-nai* had to be overcome and the issei's warrior spirit had to be recaptured.

When I was growing up in Hamilton I had known very few Japanese Canadians apart from my immediate family. In the 1980s, working in the redress movement, I discovered a whole new world of "aliens" with whom I shared an oftentimes bewildering similarity. For me, redress was a coming together of the personal and political. Lacking a physical centre or a critical population mass in Hamilton, I grew up like E.T., feeling homeless and an alien. Years later I was excited to discover that in Vancouver the community's heart was still beating, albeit faintly. There, on down-on-the-heel Powell Street, memories of old Japantown still lingered in shop windows and restaurants.

Today's Japanese Canadian community still retains vestiges of its former small-town closeness. In 1938 Charles Young wrote on Japanese Canadians: "One cannot live for weeks in the midst of a Japanese community without being impressed by their unusual loyalty to other members of their family, living or dead, and by the influence of this sentiment in determining their daily conduct. The solidarity is partly a result of the belief in 'family pedigree' which ensures the continuing influence of the family on all its members in spite of the passage of time or of separation by travel. This record is passed on from generation to generation and contains important information about all members of the family."

Perhaps that tradition explains the loyalty and long collective memory that seems to influence all our relationships. Although the community's closeness began to break down after the forced dispersal of the forties, Japanese Canadians of my mother's generation can still "place" most families they run across in the country. I remember one time years ago when I told my mother that we had hired a Japanese Canadian to do some repairs around the house, and she immediately set about to determine who the fellow was. Then with all seriousness she warned my husband to be careful. It turned out that a century earlier in Japan a member of the fellow's family had been a thief. A besmirched family honour had stained its descendants forever.

Within my community the collective memory, homogeneity, and "family" ties overlay and strengthen the cultural necessity for concensus. There is the deeply imbedded belief dating back to the founding of the imperial dynasty that we are all one family, descendants of Emperor Jimmu. Thus, no matter what transpires, in the end we must attempt to live together in a certain harmony.

Yet we also had divisions to overcome, divisions that were deeply psychological. Certainly, initially the community was severely fragmented in its attitude towards the war years. Many of the internees wanted to forget the trauma of the 1940s. Others were afraid of a possible racist backlash if Japanese Canadians were to organize and become militant. Across the country, within the community the issue was hotly debated and there were deep ruptures.

Coming to terms with the war years was distressful for the community and for each individual. In the end it was a necessary step for our mental health. Initially there were feelings of denial and self-doubt. Perhaps we had somehow deserved the hardships? Then the growing response: the government was wrong. They even knew it at the time. Their own advisers told them that there was no military necessity for the removal and internment of the Japanese Canadian community. The action was taken for purely racist and opportunistic reasons. There was no altruism. It was not done to protect us.

During the 1940s most Japanese Canadians had naively placed their trust in their Canadian leaders. Even decades later the betrayal was difficult to confront. Many felt like an adult who was sexually abused as a child and has to face both the act of incest and the parent as perpetrator. The moment was fraught with shattered trust and incredible sadness for the damage done and for what could have been. Then came the rage: rage that would propel the redress movement towards a just settlement.

Initially some members of the NAJC's National Council had supported the George Imai-led *shikataga-nai* approach, which opposed individual compensation. Others would spend over a year trying to win over this splinter group so that the community could speak with one voice. The often angry exchanges led, in September 1984, to the dissolution of Imai's redress committee during a tumultuous NAJC Redress Conference held in Toronto. The NAJC, unable to control George Imai, was "upset" by his continuation of talks with Collenette regarding a government proposal that consisted of an acknowledgement of injustices tied to the $5 million fund "to fight racism in Canada."[10] In the end Imai and his handful of *shikataga-nai* supporters left to form their own rump opposition organization, which they called the National Redress Committee of Survivors.

The year 1984 marked a watershed for the NAJC. The National Council, with its elected representatives from the community's fifteen centres across the country, elected sansei Art Miki of Winnipeg as president. In selecting Art, the national organization had made the decision to seek real justice. The National Council instructed Art to set up a strategy team that would draw up the association's redress package and negotiate an "honourable and meaningful" settlement with the recently elected Mulroney government.[11] All important decisions of the strategy team (mostly sansei) were brought back to National Council (nisei) for approval. The community representatives debated the strategy team's proposal,

and after months of discussion – often carried on by country-wide telephone conference calls – National Council agreed on the final terms:
government acknowledgement of wrongdoing; restoration of citizenship
to those expelled to Japan; removal of criminal records for offences under
the War Measures Act; $25,000 to each living Japanese Canadian
affected by the government's actions; $50 million towards a community
development fund; the amendment of the War Measures Act to prevent a
reoccurrence; and the establishment of a Human Rights Foundation to
combat racism. In November 1984, the NAJC published these demands
in *Democracy Betrayed* and presented the document to the Mulroney government.

To reassure the community that its leaders had not lost their heads,
the NAJC had to explain its program and win consensus. First on the
agenda was the reconstruction of our scattered community through the
establishment of a national communications network. The two existing
Japanese Canadian papers, *The New Canadian* and the *Canada Times,*
had a small and dwindling circulation. Total readership between them
was about five or six thousand subscribers. The NAJC decided to publish
its own paper, and by 1988 the *NAJC News* was going to one out of every
three of the country's fifty-five thousand Japanese Canadians. We
estimated that every Japanese Canadian adult in the entire country either
received a copy directly or was related to someone who did.

Our goal was to rebuild morale and bring in new supporters to the
cause. An immediate strategy was to educate and inform. Across the
country, in private homes, the NAJC conducted small informal get-
togethers to talk about the war years and the community's responsibility
to the past as well as the future. We also held regular open forums in large
auditoriums and cultural evenings that took advantage of the many artists in our community who supported the campaign.

In April 1986 the NAJC conducted a national poll of Japanese Canadians and the results indicated strong support for compensation as a
component of a redress package. In part the new militancy was brought
about because of encouraging developments in the United States. In 1983
a bi-partisan Congressional Committee had criticized the wartime
Roosevelt government for its "failure of political leadership" and recommended a payment of $20,000 to each affected Japanese American. In
1985, the report resulted in Bill 446 being introduced into the House of
Representatives. The dramatic events south of the border ignited hopes

that the Canadian government would feel compelled to react in kind. For the first time in decades, Japanese Canadian spirits were buoyed by the dream of winning justice within their lifetimes. The community members crying "Backlash" were silenced by the weekly growth of white support. Redress was in the air. As in the 1940s and early 1950s, the NAJC had become relevant to the Japanese Canadian community. The NAJC's representatives began again to speak with some authority on behalf of all of the country's Japanese Canadians.

In our initial dealings with government we had an especially large major hurdle to overcome. We had to demonstrate that the NAJC was the Japanese Canadian community's only political representative and that the NAJC's demands were one and the same as the community's. Government officials had repeatedly warned that until there was a clear consensus they wouldn't deal with the issue.[12] Divisions within the community were a god-sent excuse for government inaction.

Nowhere in Canada was the battle for community hegemony more acrimonious than in the Toronto area, which at the time had the largest number of Japanese Canadians and a majority of internment camp survivors. Yet most of Toronto's Japanese Canadians were uncomfortable with conflict and desirous of consensus. In late 1982, aware of the deep schism within the community, lawyers Shin Imai, Marcia Matsui, and I, along with a motley crew of other Japanese Canadian lawyers, writers, and artists, founded the *sodan-kai*, or the group to reach consensus.[13]

We held our first important public meeting on May 15, 1983, and hundreds came to hear Min Yasui, chair of the Japanese American Citizens' League, George Imai of the National Redress Committee, and Gordon Kadota, NAJC president. For the majority this was their first opportunity to hear first-hand about the possibilities for redress in the United States and Canada. Thereafter, the *sodan-kai* grew by leaps and bounds until most of Toronto's former nisei activists from the 1940s and the community's public figures came to our open meetings. Most in *sodan* supported the NAJC's position and opposed the group I called the *shikataganai*, but our goal was to encourage a thorough community debate in an attempt to reach consensus.

Sodan organized a series of open forums and house meetings. The public gatherings were packed, and initially members of the *shikataganai* showed up to criticize the NAJC as being too militant, too greedy, and too revengeful. However it clearly became apparent that the nay-sayers were in a minority. The overwhelming majority wanted genuine compensation and legal protections against a reoccurrence of the war-time injustice. Time and again members of the audience stood up and demanded that the NAJC put civil rights guarantees front and centre in our redress platform.

Over a period of several years *sodan* evolved into the Toronto chapter of the NAJC, strongly opposing the *shikataga-nai* faction, which was headquartered in Toronto. In spite of the fierce animosity between the two groups, both demanded that the government apologize and make financial restitution to the community. We disagreed, though, on the issues of civil rights protection and individual compensation. True to their soft line early on, in April 1985, the *shikataga-nai* dropped their demand for civil rights protections because of the "difficulties of achieving this end." [14]

The "split" in the community was then reduced to the amount and distribution of financial compensation. The question was simply, should we accept the offer of a token community award or should we demand individual payments to each survivor? In reality the compensation disagreement masked a psychological division: *Yamato* (warrior spirit) versus *shikataga-nai* (resignation). Could the community summon forth and sustain a difficult and long battle with the government? Or had our walking-wounded mentality been too deeply fashioned into our souls?

In early 1985 the NAJC strategy team had been presented with a take it or leave it offer of some $5 million to $6 million. After the NAJC team rejected this ultimatum from the Mulroney government it was hounded by the press and the government to disclose a bottom-line figure. Although the U.S. community's demand of $25,000 per survivor had been common knowledge for several years, Japanese Canadians were initially afraid to publicly demand compensation of that magnitude. From the beginning white allies had come to our defence when they learned about our unjust treatment during the war. We feared losing this support if our claim was seen to be unreasonable.

Nonetheless, in 1985, after considerable soul searching, the NAJC announced publicly that we were seeking $25,000 per survivor. The government quickly calculated that this totalled some $350 million dollars, given twelve thousand possible beneficiaries. There was a slight gasp and some softening of editorial and public support at this disclosure. However, the dire *shikataga-nai* predictions of racist backlash failed to materialize and consequently the community's anxieties waned. The *shikataganai's* activities became limited to shrill denunciations of the NAJC in the community press.

To demonstrate that our refusal of the government's offer was rational, and to make our case more palatable to the Canadian public, the NAJC decided in late 1984 to hire a well-known independent third party to determine the amount of damages suffered by the community. Although we knew that the government had all the necessary information in the national archives and that we could prepare such a report ourselves, we believed that Canadians would find it more credible if the documentation was prepared by a respected impartial body.

Unfortunately, all too quickly we discovered that the cost of hiring a top-flight firm was considerably out of our price range. The NAJC was an impoverished voluntary organization, whose national office was the dining-room table of our president, Art Miki. Fortunately, through the Vancouver grapevine we heard that Phil Barter, a senior partner at Price Waterhouse, might be sympathetic. I discovered that the sixty-year-old Barter, a socially concerned, physically dominating six-foot-nine man, was also a person with a hidden past.

When Phil was a child of preschool age he befriended Misaro Ito and Tadesco Kagetsu, two neighbourhood Japanese Canadian boys. As children do, they often ate at each other's homes. Phil recalls that he tried his first sushi then, prepared by the boys' grandmothers. He also remembers, with emotional difficulty, the spring day in April 1942 when together with his parents and sisters he went to see his two boyhood friends off at the Vancouver CPR station. Child enemy aliens, they were headed for internment camps in the Kootenays. He recalls at eight years of age being bewildered about why his chums had suddenly become his enemies. His father, a moral man and a First World War veteran who had fought with Japanese Canadian soldiers, was asked to be a local militia chief, and refused. The senior Barter was furious that his neighbours were being held in Canadian prison camps.

The morning that Phil's two childhood friends boarded the train that would take them out of his life was etched in his memory forever. The steam locomotive train was pulling a line of cars packed with Japanese

Canadian families and their worldly possessions. The Barters brought small presents for their neighbours, which with today's hindsight Phil now acknowledges was a mistake. Japanese custom would require a mutual exchange of gifts, and given the circumstances this was impossible. Although Phil's father visited the Ito and Kagetsu families in the internment camps during the war, Phil was never to see his friends again. The memory of the injustice remained, however, throughout the years.

Phil Barter recalls that the staff at Price Waterhouse had previously "tossed around" the problem of putting a dollar figure to the Japanese Canadian community's losses of the 1940s. When he was approached by a delegation from the Vancouver Japanese Canadian community headed by business associate Henry Wakabayashi, memories of the wrong done so many years before resurfaced. Wanting in his own way to amend the past, Phil went out on a limb and assured the Japanese Canadian representatives that his firm would be pleased to undertake the project. Telling the NAJC "not to worry about the money," he later obtained the unanimous approval of the other members of the company's executive board to perform the work on a contingency basis at cost, with some of the legwork to be done by the NAJC.

Still, a difficult and pressing problem remained: to prove to the media and the government that the NAJC represented the Japanese Canadians. Both continued to portray the community as divided and on that basis failed to treat the NAJC or its demands seriously. Although largely marginalized within the community, nonetheless the *shikataga-nai* continued to assert to a willingly believing government and press that they represented the "surviving silent majority." Exposing the falsity of their claims was as difficult as shadowboxing a phantom because the *shikataga-nai* purposefully avoided public confrontations with the NAJC. To compound the problem, the NAJC's National Council, in true Japanese fashion, refused to respond to its opponents' vituperative attacks in the community papers.

But the community was beginning to find support from outsiders. On January 28, 1985, through an intervention introduced by a friend, alderman Dale Martin, Toronto City Council unanimously passed a motion encouraging the Mulroney government "to continue negotiations with the NAJC to attempt to reach an amicable settlement of redress for Japanese Canadians."

As our negotiations with Jack Murta, the minister responsible for our portfolio, were at a standstill, I spoke with members of the Toronto Mayor's Committee on Community and Race Relations (MCCRR). I informed them that the NAJC planned to retain the respected accounting firm of Price Waterhouse to prepare an economic study of the wartime Japanese Canadian losses and to establish that the NAJC's rejection of the government's offer of $6 million was based on the acknowledged principle that the amount of compensation paid should bear some relationship to the losses suffered. Knowing that we lacked funds for such a project, the MCCRR proposed that Toronto City Council provide the NAJC with a grant of $5,000 towards defraying the Price Waterhouse bill. The resolution also proposed that Toronto "communicate with all other members of the Federation of Canadian Municipalities urging them to accept the urgency of the situation and to make appropriate contributions immediately."

News of the proposed Toronto City Council's resolution reached the *shikataga-nai,* who wrote Mayor Art Eggleton opposing the grant to the NAJC. The *shikataga-nai* claimed that they represented the Toronto Japanese Canadian community and opposed the city's financial donation and endorsation of the NAJC. In support they appended a list of some twenty-five community individuals and organizations that, they asserted, recognized their leadership.

Despite Council's January motion, the City Clerk informed me that before they would proceed any further, Council needed to know which organization spoke for the Japanese Canadian community. Both sides were instructed to send delegations to the MCCRR for a full airing of the matter. Within the community the *shikataga-nai* strategy had been to avoid public showdowns with the NAJC, so not surprisingly the *shikataga-nai* faction requested a private in-camera hearing.

The Toronto MCCRR hearing afforded our side its first real opportunity to expose the *shikataga-nai.* It was crucial that the NAJC receive the official recognition of Toronto City Council. As the NAJC's Toronto legal counsel, I prepared for the hearing as if for an important trial. I knew that if the *shikataga-nai* was recognized by the country's most important municipal government as representing Toronto's Japanese Canadian community, the NAJC's redress struggle would be kneecapped. Such a decision would have left the Conservative government free to recognize the *shikataga-nai* as the national voice of Japanese Canadians. The Tories would then have been able, as they hoped – and with little public recrimination – to quickly issue an apology and a $5-million "memorialization" to close that chapter in Canadian history. However, if Toronto City Council decided that the NAJC spoke for the Japanese Canadian community, the federal government would be forced to recognize us and deal with our claim. The press could no longer cover the story as simply another internal ethnic spat but as an issue between the whole Japanese Canadian community and the federal government. It would also clear the way for white organizations that had wanted to condemn the wartime activities but had been uncertain about which Japanese Canadian faction to support.

We in the Toronto NAJC chapter[15] knew that the emperor had no clothes. The Toronto *shikataga-nai*, through its organization the Toronto Japanese Canadian Citizens' Association (TJCCA), had not held a democratic election or called a public meeting in years. Their executive, consisting of a handful of individuals, met in a downtown Japanese restaurant or in the supply room of the Japanese Canadian Cultural Centre in Don Mills. We knew that their list of followers was a figment of their imagination. In preparation for the public hearing, members of the Toronto NAJC chapter approached each of the organizations cited by our opponents. Quickly a dosier of declarations was compiled from individuals and organizations that denied supporting the *shikataga-nai* faction. In a majority of cases, executive members of the organizations stated that they recognized the NAJC as the community's sole political representative. In fact there was "no evidence" to support Imai's claim that his group had seven thousand members in ten centres across the country. When asked by a *Globe and Mail* reporter, Imai could not name one Vancouver supporter.[16]

On May 28, 1985, armed with a briefcase stuffed with papers and surrounded by a standing-room-only crowd, I made the NAJC's case before the Mayor's Committee. After hearing both sides, the Committee recommended that Toronto City Council support the NAJC and its grant application. By the time I had addressed the neighbourhoods and finance committees there remained no doubt that the *shikataga-nai* had been officially discredited.

On May 16, 1985, the NAJC had announced that we had hired Price

Waterhouse to undertake a socio-economic study of the wartime losses. Economists Bob Elton and Martin Roberts would supervise the research and write the report. On August 12, 1985, Toronto City Council passed its resolution and donated $5,000 towards the NAJC's Price Waterhouse study. Council deemed that the purpose of the grant was "in the interest of the Municipality."

This victory for the NAJC had important ramifications within the Japanese Canadian community. Word of Toronto City Council's support spread quickly. For an apprehensive minority filled with timid souls, fearful of a racist backlash, it was like a shot in the arm. Toronto's support for the NAJC was matched in March 1986 by the City of Vancouver and in June 1986 by Lethbridge City Council.

These political endorsations from the country's important municipal governments worked hand in hand to rebuild the community's confidence and the forging of concensus. As cautious Japanese Canadians began to see that white Canadians supported a negotiated redress settlement, they began to openly side with the NAJC. Now, in retrospect it seems that those who opposed redress either publicly or privately did so more out of trepidation than principle. In any case, as evidence of widespread support across the country grew with each passing day, fearful Japanese Canadians gained courage.

A year later Price Waterhouse issued its findings. The firm concluded that the community's income and property losses alone were at least $443 million in 1986 dollars. They made no attempt to estimate the financial cost occasioned by the breakup of families or by the loss of liberty and civil rights during the years of internment, exile, and dispersal. In the community, at least, the tide had turned. On the evening of April 1, 1986, the City of Toronto and the Toronto NAJC co-sponsored an event in City Council chambers to commemorate what was to become the first of our "Freedom Day" celebrations. The day was the anniversary of April 1, 1949, which marked the ending of all wartime restrictions against Japanese Canadians and gave us, for the first time in our history, the same rights of citizenship as white Canadians.

That night in 1986, as Toronto Japanese Canadians were greeted at City Hall by the Mayor's representative, many felt for the first time since they had been relocated to Toronto that they were truly being welcomed to the city. Some still remembered the days in the 1940s when Toronto, fearing our contamination, refused us entry. At this happy event, the overflow crowd included not only Japanese Canadians but also official representatives from many of Toronto's other ethnic communities. Redress was becoming a Canadian issue. The faint mirage of the *Yamato* spirit was growing more visible.

6 | Legal Pawns of Fate

It is the first step which costs; an injustice once performed is
fatally easy to repeat.

Saturday Night, April, 1947
on the treatment of Japanese Canadians

DESPITE A CULTURAL abhorrence of the courts, the issei had been compelled over the years to sue the Canadian government in efforts to change
the myriad of discriminatory laws that had chained them to second-class
status. Traditionally Japanese hold everyone involved in a conflict partly
responsible for it. There is a common saying that even a thief is thirty per
cent right. To this day it is through mutual apology and compromise that
the Japanese strive to avoid the public notoriety of a law suit.

Still, in the 1980s what held the NAJC back from launching a flurry of
legal motions was not cultural heritage or a scarcity of lawyers, because
the association had an arsenal of litigious-happy sansei lawyers who had
volunteered their services. As sixties activists, many of us, myself
included, had gone to law school in part motivated by the rhetoric of the
day to become "lawyers for the people." As a result, the Japanese Canadian redress movement was top-heavy with sansei lawyers with a common vision: to use the law to bring about justice.

During the 1970s and 1980s, my counterparts in the United States were busy suing the government and bringing forward constitutional arguments. Enviously we watched their ingenious motions and plotted our own strategies. Over the years we left few stones unturned in our quest, though in the end we had little to show for our efforts except calloused hands. Our brush with the legal system would ultimately play a minor role in our victory. Sadly, we discovered that our well-documented, dismal history before the Canadian and English courts was a mighty precedent that, like a heavy weight, kept us in our place.

My own sense of powerlessness before the courts and legal system was personified by the story of Akihide Otsuji. In 1948 Aki, an eighteen-year-old boy, had been sentenced to a year's hard labour for returning to British Columbia's coast. Covering Aki's trial in 1948, *Vancouver Sun* columnist Jack Scott wrote: "There was no great outcry of protest when this boy left the court room. The magistrate gave no indication that this was a case with deep roots of intolerance and bigotry. Indeed, there had been no counsel for the boy. He had conducted his own case in a pathetic and ludicrous manner. It was all over in five minutes. An open and shut case. The evidence against him was simply that he was a person of the Japanese race."[1]

When I first read about Aki in Ken Adachi's *The Enemy That Never Was*, I was shocked by our silent history with its unknown victims and heroes.[2] For me, Adachi's book was like the unlocking of an old rusted cellar door. Suddenly I had entered into a hidden, stench-filled room. Intrigued by Aki's case, I gradually pieced together the story from bits of information I came across over the years. One time I was told that Aki had spent much of his prison term weeping inconsolably. Angered, I felt that only the antiseptic light of day and the burning heat of the sun's rays could cleanse that boy's cell.

Aki's sister Mary told me that before the war their mother had taken the youngest children to Japan to attend a family marriage and had got stuck there after Pearl Harbour. Upon receiving the relocation orders, their father and the rest of the family, including Aki, were moved to Coaldale, Alberta, to work on a sugar-beet farm. In 1946, faced with the government's ultimatum to move further east or to Japan, Aki's father, believing that his wife and young children would not be allowed to return to Canada, decided to try to keep the family together by relocating to

Japan. Only Aki chose to remain in Canada. Soon afterwards, alone and desperate, sixteen-year-old Aki followed his family to Vancouver, but it was too late to arrange his passage to Japan. He went underground in Vancouver, posing as a Chinaman until he was picked up by the police and put on trial. His crime? Japanese Canadians had been banned from returning to within one hundred miles of the west coast until April 1, 1949. Mary said that Aki spent much of his year in jail in the "hole" and that the experience contributed to a further decline after his release. His life thereafter became a revolving door of institutional care.

During the 1950s Aki's family gradually returned to Canada. The last time that Mary saw her brother was in 1977, when he confided to her that he had been warned that if he had any relatives his disability pension would be cut off. A decade later his dead body was found by his landlord in a seedy Seymour Street rooming house. The cause of death, I was told, was an aneurysm of an ulcer. For a long time his sister, friends in Vancouver say, was embarrassed to speak of him. She was ashamed of this lost soul who, with cast down eyes, wandered on Powell Street and slept in the flea-bag hotels of Vancouver's old Japantown. Long and hard, Mary worked on Vancouver's Redress Committee.

For years Aki has been in my thoughts. During a criminal trial, when a judge seemed particularly racist or inhuman, I would think of him. My teenage clients seemed more hardened and street-wise than eighteen-year-old Aki was said to have been, but I thought I could see the same kind of fear on their young faces and hear the same bravado in their falsetto macho voices.

At one time I suggested to the NAJC that we try to have Aki's case reopened. In 1985 I met with sansei American Japanese San Francisco Bay area lawyers who were working on several appeals. The U.S. lawyers were eventually successful in "expunging" the 1940s criminal convictions for curfew violations of Japanese Americans Min Yasui and Gordon Hirabayashi. I thought of Aki. Perhaps if we were able to "expunge" his record, it would make him whole again. Further legal research indicated that the remedy of "expungement" is non-existent in Canada. Our closest equivalent is the pardon, but the connotation of a pardon is completely different. It admits no error on the part of either the courts or the state. Instead it portrays the image of a generous and gracious government that forgives a sinner who has recanted or otherwise redeemed his past life and who upon close examination is now fit to rejoin the good folk of society.

Since the NAJC wanted an unequivocal admission of wrongdoing by the courts and the state, we didn't pursue the case. However, one of the terms of the settlement that the NAJC negotiated with the government allows for those who have convictions under the War Measures Act to obtain pardons if they so wish. I suspect that because almost all of those who were incarcerated were held without charges, trials, or convictions, few if any Japanese Canadians will take advantage of this provision. Nonetheless Aki's sister Mary had planned to apply for a pardon for him, but she found there is no provision for granting a pardon posthumously.

It is my sorrow that I never had the chance to meet Aki. He died alone in 1987, a year before Prime Minister Mulroney admitted that the war time actions taken against Canadians of Japanese ancestry were "unjust ... and influenced by discriminatory attitudes."

Even with our community's formidably depressing legal batting average – or perhaps because of it – the sansei lawyers steeped in the civil rights rhetoric of the 1960s were keen to bring our issue before the courts. Idealistically, we hoped to win a ringing victory from the country's highest court or, better yet, enshrine in the Constitution effective guarantees that would limit the power of the state and protect those who for whatever reason were the social pariahs of the day. Over a period of five years the Japanese Canadian legal team researched various possibilities. During this period it seemed we were always crumpling a good idea into a ball and tossing it into the wastepaper basket. Ultimately we were to discover that, like the issei and nisei before us, we also lacked the power to win in court.

WAR MEASURES ACT (WMA)

Time and again at public gatherings or at meetings of the National Council, the community's venom was directed against the WMA because it had nefariously provided the government with a legal blanket to cover its dirty deeds of the 1940s. This searing memory caused the NAJC in the early 1980s to establish a WMA Committee that was initially headed by a Hamilton urology professor, Dr. Art Shimizu. Other members were lawyers Shin Imai and Alan Hoyano, Hamilton artist Bryce Kanbara, and myself. By the mid-1980s the committee's work would be taken over by the NAJC legal team, but in the meantime we considered two options: abolition or amendment.

Abolition would mean that Canada would have no emergency legislation, which is the situation in some democratic countries, such as the former West Germany. There a parliamentary emergency committee including representatives of various regions of the country was empowered to declare an emergency by a two-thirds vote. But there were problems with this approach too, depending on your faith in politicians. Some of us thought that under stress the government could overreact and pass legislation that would unnecessarily trample civil rights. Others, perhaps more generously, speculated that cabinet could indeed draft an act tailored to adequately fit the seriousness of the situation, but that this process would eat into valuable time required to deal with the emergency.

Option two was an amended, new improved WMA. This alternative was based on the principle that it is better to know your enemy. The movement to amend the existing WMA to incorporate civil rights protections and restrict the anti-democratic powers of cabinet was an old one. In 1979 a Canadian Civil Liberties Association brief to the McDonald Commission of Inquiry into RCMP activities proposed that Parliament be empowered to regularly review orders-in-council passed pursuant to the WMA.

Understandably, one of our longstanding criticisms of the WMA was its limited compensation provisions to innocent victims. This was a restriction we wanted to see changed in any new or amended act. Given our own community's experience we were surprised when we were told by Quebec civil rights lawyers that after the FLQ "crisis" of October 1970, damages had been paid to those who had been unjustly picked up and jailed in the blanket sweep of the Quebec separatist movement. This discovery led us in October 1986 to Penny Simpson, who had been a Montreal political activist during the October crisis. In a letter to Art Miki, Simpson wrote that under the draconian powers of the WMA she had been held incommunicado for one week in Montreal's Tanguay prison for women. Afterwards she was fired from her job because of her "notoriety." She received $600 in compensation for her financial losses from the Quebec government. Interestingly, the province had admitted responsibility for imposing the WMA, a federal statute.

In the early 1980s the NAJC Council discussed the various options. In the end, Council decided to abandon the WMA and press instead for constitutional guarantees that would ensure that our experience could not be repeated regardless of what emergency legislation was on the books. In the following years, during our negotiation meetings with various multicultural ministers, the NAJC lawyers continued to raise the question of the WMA. Like harassed parents dealing with troublesome children, the government representatives always told us that our concerns were being taken under advisement, that the government was planning on introducing new legislation, and that this was not just a Japanese Canadian issue.

Finally, in 1988, after years of speculation, the government brought in a draft emergency powers act. Amazingly, when it came time to hear public deputations on the bill the NAJC was not invited to make a presentation to the all-party committee – a surprising turn of affairs because we were convinced that WMA-2 appeared on the Tory agenda at least partly because of our redress campaign. We also felt that of all Canadians we were living experts on the excessive powers of the old WMA. Through backroom manoeuvring orchestrated by opposition members of the Commons on our behalf, and with the threat that the NAJC would go to the press if we were not allowed to speak, the government relented and finally "invited" the NAJC to address the committee. Ottawa lawyer Ann Gomer Sunahara, the author of The Politics of Racism, co-ordinated the community's brief, which recommended that even in an emergency the government should not be allowed to override the equality sections of the Charter and that compensation provisions should be included in the new act.[3]

Perrin Beatty, the Minister of National Defence, had been made aware of the Japanese Canadian community's fears. He wrote to Art Miki that he appreciated our "wish to be reassured" that Bill C-77 (the new Emergency Powers Act) did not permit the Governor-in-Council (cabinet) to override the Charter of Rights and Freedoms. He added, "I am advised that there is very little basis for concern on this point."[4] Miki urged Beatty to refer this important question for decision to the Supreme Court of Canada.[5] During our final August 1988 negotiation sessions, the government representatives proudly pointed to the new Emergencies Act as positive proof of their commitment to civil rights. The cabinet ministers said that having gone through the public scrutiny of the requisite parliamentary public hearings, they felt confident that the excesses of the past could not be repeated. They pointed out that the new emergency legislation contained a compensation procedure that would be followed in cases of internments or property confiscations.

With good reason the Japanese Canadian community has always been sceptical of government reassurances. We will always fear that in an emergency the country may be ruled by men who care little for the civil rights of its citizens.

CHARTER OF RIGHTS AND FREEDOMS

Early in 1984, Vancouver lawyer Don Rosenbloom, a specialist in aboriginal land claims, became an adviser to the NAJC legal/strategy team. Through his marriage to Michiko, a dynamic Japanese immigrant, community activist, and businesswoman, Rosenbloom was sensitive to our past. During the years of our struggle, he would provide us with much appreciated advice. As well, we profited from Rosenbloom's association with Tom Berger, the former B.C. Supreme Court Justice, who was willing to act as a sounding board for the NAJC strategy team. Almost from the beginning Rosenbloom urged the NAJC to stop focusing on the WMA and to instead concentrate our energies on the Constitution. Rosenbloom correctly reasoned that the WMA as an act of Parliament could easily be amended and repealed (as indeed it was in 1988). He argued that the Constitution, the supreme law of the land, would in the long run provide Canadians with the most secure form of civil rights protections.

As legal counsel to Native associations during the constitutional debates in the early 1980s, Rosenbloom had been privy to some of the backroom political discussions. From this exposure he predicted that the NAJC would most likely be unsuccessful in any attempt to limit the constitutional powers of the federal or provincial governments. As a fallback position Rosenbloom supported the strategy of lobbying for the inclusion in the Constitution of an ethnic minority protection clause (similar to section 28, the women's equality provision). We all thought, wrongly as it happened, that politically both the federal and provincial governments would find it difficult to oppose such a motherhood amendment. [6]

In June 1985 a Special Parliamentary Committee on Equality Rights was passing through town to hear from "ordinary Canadians." Always optimistic about the democratic process, the NAJC asked me to appear before this committee to make our constitutional arguments. Afterwards, apart from the form letter thanking the NAJC for its valuable contribution, nothing more came from this government consultative process. However, as word seeped out that the NAJC was pushing for constitutional amendments, civil libertarians warned of the possible dangers. They cautioned that once the lid was off the jack-in-the-box, the right-wing business lobby would use the occasion to argue for the dismantling of the country's social welfare and labour protections. Fearful of the conservative times, they counselled that constitutional talks would only result in the further erosion of people's rights.

Inside the NAJC, one such debate centred on the pros and cons of lobbying for constitutional "private property" protections. Based on the U.S. experience, some people in our community thought that if we had had the same constitutional guarantees as the American Japanese the Canadian government would not have been able to seize all our property. But tenant activists, aboriginal rights supporters, and family law experts advised that such an amendment, if given a traditional narrow legal interpretation, would seriously undermine the gains that tenants, Natives, and women had made. At the time it appeared that the only pressure groups in the country backing the entrenchment of property rights in the Constitution were the Toronto developers and *The Toronto Sun*. We quietly dropped the issue. And in the end it turned out that the question of a Charter amendment or challenge was totally academic – like all of our constitutional considerations.

PUBLIC INQUIRY

Our community's only exposure to Royal Commissions had been the Henry Bird Inquiry in the late 1940s, which looked into property losses suffered by Japanese Canadians. Many of our people had been embittered by that experience.

We were not oblivious, though, to the positive benefits of the recent U.S. Commission into the wartime treatment of Japanese Americans. During the early 1980s the U.S. Commission had acted as a catalyst within the American Japanese community. It had educated white Americans about a closed chapter of their history and provided positive nationwide publicity. Most importantly, in 1983 the bipartisan Commission had issued its findings. Chairperson Joan Bernstein, speaking from the congressional Commission's unanimous report, said that the U.S. government's actions had been motivated by "race prejudice, war hysteria and the failure of political leadership."[7] The Report recommended a congressional apology; the establishment of a $1.5 billion fund to compensate the sixty thousand survivors at $20,000 per internee, with the remainder going into a community fund; pardons to all American Japanese who had been convicted of curfew and detention violations; and restitution for lost benefits to all American Japanese who had been civil servants during the war period.[8]

Enviously, the NAJC strategy team considered lobbying for a parallel Canadian inquiry. We theorized that Canadians would be moved by the testimony of Japanese Canadians and educated about racism. We hoped that the hearings would create a citizenry critical of anti-democratic government actions. For a time some members of the strategy team, swept away by the remarkable U.S. Commission's recommendations, argued forcibly for this option. However, when the idea was reviewed under the cold harsh light of Canadian realpolitik it was abandoned. Though we were political neophytes we still realized that unlike our "cousins" to the south we lacked the political clout required to have input into the composition and terms of reference of a government commission. We also recognized that the federal government would stack the panel with their friends, not ours, and that our community would be forever stuck with its recommendations.

No doubt we would have been happiest with the results of an NAJC-mounted inquiry, but that kind of undertaking would have cost us several million dollars, money we did not have; and its suggestions would probably have been ignored or at best shelved by the government. At a meeting held in Vancouver on November 3, 1984, the strategy committee, which at that time consisted of Art Miki, his brother Roy, Ritz Inouye, Jerry Hisaoka, and myself, recommended to NAJC Council that we directly negotiate with the Tories and abandon the Royal Commission route.

Interestingly enough, years later, in 1988, during our final negotiations with Gerry Weiner and Lucien Bouchard, government officials confided that they wished in hindsight that Canada had struck a commission similar to the one in the United States. They believed that the process of holding hearings around the country to fully air the facts would have been educational. Although they worried that the bigots would have come out of the woodwork, just as they did in the United States, they trusted that on fully hearing the facts Canadians, like Americans, would have been horrified by the actions taken by their government against innocent citizens and would have had no hesitation in supporting the case for redress.

STATED CASE OR DECLARATION

For the longest time, while working in the redress movement we often seemed to come up against one dead end after another. A case in point occurrred in March 1985, when I met with Toronto lawyer Andrew Roman, the national director of the Public Interest Advocacy Centre. At the time, consumer activists described him as Canada's Ralph Nader and lawyer friends had told me that he was interested in our case.

Walking up the stairs to Roman's unpretentious offices on Yonge Street, I found myself hoping that somehow he would magically provide the key to open the courtroom doors that had been padlocked against us. For a year I had felt that the NAJC legal team was simply spinning its wheels. I was curious to hear Roman's advice. Right away Roman flatly stated that the government's current offer of $6 million was "almost irrelevant." He said that the "figure had very little to do with Canadians of Japanese origin and was simply a ploy to get our problem off of Murta's desk." As to amending the Charter, he said that the government "would not be enthusiastic about amending the Charter this early in its life for something that was not originated by the provinces or the federal government itself." Later, in a letter, he advised that if the NAJC tied its whole package to that objective, we would waste a lot of time on "fruitless negotiations."[9]

In Roman's opinion the NAJC had nine major problems to overcome: ours was an old injustice that was not well known; redress was not a hot topic (like women's rights); our injustices had happened during wartime, when extraordinary measures are imposed; it was essentially a B.C. issue and of no interest east of Ontario; it was a transitory problem because with each passing year more of the survivors would die; it was ugly because it raised the question of racism; it required a messy solution, not a simple one; the Mulroney Tories had just received a massive majority to deal with the national deficit; and, if all of that wasn't enough, the case raised several unresolved legal issues. Roman recommended that the NAJC lobby the various provincial attorneys-general to have a specific question put before the Supreme Court of Canada: would today's Charter of Rights prevent a government acting in an emergency from riding rough-shod over the rights of its citizens? This proposal – of asking the Supreme Court for a declaration – was an interesting one that we had not previously considered. Legally the proposal was up against a major obstacle – the Statute of Limitations – as well as facing several other lesser legal hurdles that we would have to overcome if we were to get before the "Supremes."

Roman arranged for me to meet with the aged reigning king of Canadian law, John J. Robinette, a lawyer of considerable reputation. It was said that in his prime Robinette had possessed the sharpest legal mind in the country. Once, I had seen him arguing a case before the Federal Court of Appeal, and it was almost as if he were speaking in his living room to friends. The members of the bench all appeared to be awake and listening – a feat in itself. A critic of the judiciary, I was duly impressed. Robinette was a partner in one of the largest and wealthiest Toronto Bay Street firms, which occupies several floors of a downtown highrise bank tower. As I crossed the threshhold I knew that usually only the firm's richest and most important clients received an audience with J.J. I wondered, does anyone even dare call him that to his face?

Roman had warned me that given his advanced years, Robinette only took cases that piqued his curiosity in some way. I anxiously prepared for our meeting as if I were getting ready for a final law school examination. Nervously I briefed Robinette on the facts, the existing law, and tried to interest him in the constitutional question that the NAJC case would pose: would the Charter of Rights protect Canadians from a reoccurrence of the WWII experience of Japanese Canadians? A small, spectacled figure, Robinette listened intently and said little. But he did let slip an interesting aside. He told me that the British North America Act, which predates the Canadian Constitution, contains a little-known section that permits the establishment of leper colonies. Presumably by inference, he said stroking his chin, this clause provided the legal justification for the internment of any social untouchables.

After a draining morning I left Robinette with a cardboard carton full of books and documents. After hearing about my audience with him, several lawyers in his firm volunteered to work *pro bono* on the research if Robinette agreed to undertake the project, Robinette declined. I never learned why.

In 1985, in a last bid to resurrect the declaration option, on impulse I telephoned Arnie Schultz, a Winnipeg legal acquaintance who was working for the Manitoba NDP government. I asked Schultz whether he thought Attorney-General Roland Penner would be interested in referring our constitutional question to the Supreme Court. Nothing came of the call.

U.N. HUMAN RIGHTS COMPLAINT

In the summer of 1985 Charles Roach, a Black activist and human rights lawyer, introduced me to his friend Bertram Ramcharam, a United Nations Human Rights Tribunal commissioner. On a long hot afternoon in Roach's backyard in downtown Toronto, the three of us discussed the potential of bringing the wartime mistreatment of Japanese Canadians before this international forum.

It had been many years since Roach and I had practised criminal law together. He had been my boss and in those days the office policy was to plead every client not guilty, which meant most had a trial. Partly as a consequence, the firm's lawyers were despised by police and crown attorneys alike, who preferred the speed and surety of plea bargaining. Then, as now, Roach could be depended on to fight for the underdog. That afternoon, Bertram Ramcharam advised me frankly that although Canada reacted very sensitively to criticisms from the international body, the Tribunal's findings could not be highly critical. After all, the event had taken place four decades ago, and compared to the complaints of genocidal wars and tortures brought regularly before the Commission the Canadian injustice was less horrific. In today's world a few deaths, suicides, years of misery, and the wrongful imprisonment of thousands would merit a mere rap on the knuckles. But Ramcharam did agree that the very act of airing our laundry in an international forum could force Mulroney back to the negotiation table.

Accordingly we strategized three procedures to get the NAJC case before the U.N. Tribunal: a complaint laid on our behalf by a recognized non-governmental organization such as Amnesty International; a "stand alone" charge alleging massive violations of human rights; or a complaint that fell within the terms of the optional protocol of the International Covenant of Civil and Political Rights. The last procedure had been used successfully in 1981 by Sandra Lovelace, a Canadian aboriginal woman who had lost her (and her children's) Native rights by marrying a white man. This Canadian law only applied to Native women and not to Native men. Four years later, embarrassed by international criticism, the Canadian government amended the Indian Act and removed this discriminatory provision.

Unfortunately, the U.N. Tribunal has no powers of enforcement. It is further limited in that it can only deal with violations that have occurred in the period after a country became a signator to the Optional Protocol, which in Canada's case was August 19, 1976. To succeed, Japanese Canadians would have to argue that the earlier, wartime violations had effects that continued into the present. As long as Mulroney's ministers continued to meet with us, the NAJC kept the U.N. complaints route in abeyance. Later, by the middle of 1987 when negotiations had come to a dead halt, I dusted off my U.N. dossier in preparation for the filing of a complaint.

LAW SUIT

In early 1988 Bob Banno, a member of the Vancouver Redress Committee and a partner in a large Vancouver law firm, arranged for the gratuitous preparation of a lengthy legal paper that outlined possible avenues for launching a law suit. Banno is the son of Dr. Edward Banno, the Vancouver dentist who in May 1936 had been one of the four nisei delegates sent to Ottawa to lobby for the franchise for Canadian-born Japanese. The Banno firm's memorandum proposed various routes that might get us around our most serious roadblock: the Statute of Limitations, which had steadfastly blocked our access to the courts. Some of the solutions proposed were ingenious, but most of them, regretfully, had already been determined against us in the past.

For years, from the sidelines, the NAJC had wistfully considered suing the government. We had silently cheered in 1983, when a group of litigious American Japanese launched, in their words, "an unambiguously adversarial" law suit for the sum of $24 billion claiming damages for false arrest and loss of civil rights for the 120,000 American Japanese who had been interned in 1942-44. The group, called the National Council for

Japanese American Redress (NCJAR) and headed by William Hohri of Chicago, was unsuccessful at getting to first base. [10] My association with Hohri, a gregarious, bow-tie-sporting, mid-western American, dates back to 1982. Since that time, intrigued by the route his group had decided to take, I have kept in touch with him.

Futilely the NCJAR had spent $200,000 trying to get the courts to hear whether the wartime U.S. government actions infringed the constitutional and civil rights of Americans. Their most serious obstacle had been the expiry of the six-year limitations period. By law litigants are required to file law suits before the expiry of the Statute of Limitations. After that it's like trying to get a manufacturer to honour an out-of-date warranty.

NCJAR unsuccessfully argued that because the U.S. government had "engaged in 'affirmative acts of concealment and fraud' ... that the government should be 'estopped' [prevented] from raising the defense of the statute of limitations." [11] In some environmental and industrial injury cases, where certain key information has come into the hands of the victims after the ending of the six-year period, courts have ignored the statutory bar. Adding strength to the NCJAR claim was the fact that much of the damning information implicating the government has been protected by the Official Secrets Act, which shields sensitive government material for thirty years. Nonetheless the U.S. Supreme Court, relying primarily on the Statute of Limitations, threw the case out in 1987.

Legally, we in Canada would have had to overcome the same limitations hurdle. For the sake of argument, even if the NAJC had succeeded on that point, thereafter we would have been on much thinner ice. Until 1949 Japanese Canadians were denied the rights of citizenship and up to 1982 Canadians had no constitutional protections.

Sadly, the NAJC was aware that in the United States, the NCJAR, even as *pro bono* clients of a Washington, D.C., civil rights firm, nevertheless had to raise $200,000 to pay the costs of its suit and that years of litigation had been tied up in procedural matters on the Statute of Limitations question. Nonetheless, for me the most interesting suggestion put forward by Banno's firm was the proposal that the NAJC seek a declaration as to "personal status" – namely, that we ask the courts to find improper the deportation decision of 1947 that blurred the distinction between Canadian-born Japanese and aliens. Because this Supreme

Court decision could still affect citizenship rights, perhaps, the thinking went, the Court might suspend the Statute of Limitations bar.

The lawyers in Banno's firm proposed to work for out-of-pocket expenses, with the bulk of their fee being billed on a contingency basis. They predicted that a law suit could last five years and might end up costing a million dollars. Their proposal was brought to NAJC Council for a decision by dedicated Vancouver strategy-team member and lawyer Cassandra Kobayashi. The response of National Council was that given the risks the legal route was too rich for our blood. We also knew that in 1987 the U.S. House of Representatives had passed Bill HR442, which proposed to award $20,000 in compensation to each of the sixty thousand Japanese American survivors. The sources in our U.S. counterpart, the Japanese American Citizens' League, informed us that the bill was going to the Senate in the spring of 1988. Crossing our fingers, National Council decided to await the outcome south of the border.

In the end, I viewed our legal schemes as akin to buying lottery tickets. We could dream of winning in court, but realistically our chances of success were the same as being hit by lightning. Although we were rich in young lawyers who were itching to fight it out in the courts, we were also sadly aware that we faced a century of legal precedents and an unsympathetic judiciary. Legal justice would have required a very inventive bench concerned about the rights of racial minorities. Sadly, to date no such court has existed in this country. With the recent appointment of women to Canada's highest court, the "Supremes" are becoming more aware of the rights and concerns of fifty-two per cent of the country's population. But although justice is embodied as a blindfolded woman, Canada's all-white court has rarely been colour blind when it comes to Native or Japanese Canadian rights. In the end, the NAJC decided that we had a greater likelihood of winning justice not from a bench filled with rich white lawyers but from a jury of our peers. We resolved to take our case to the Canadian people.

7 | In the Corridors of Power: 1984-88

Combat makes apparent
something that already exists.
A battle is always won
before it begins,
since it is won in the mind.

– Miyamoto Musashi *The Book of Five Rings*, 1643

THERE IS A KIND of seamlessness about the story of our four years of
negotiations with a string of Tory multiculturalism ministers. The ministers seemed to be assigned mainly to get us off the government's back. We
were prepared to hang on, oftentimes by our fingernails. Having decided
to challenge the past, we immediately found ourselves thrown into a
psychological boxing ring with masters of manipulation. The various
federal ministers of multiculturalism made us painfully aware of our legal
impotence and political insignificance. As we were being ushered into
their airless chambers for a negotiation session we would be knocked off
balance by an offhand putdown. For me personally it became important
to overcome feelings of discomfort and weakness. Through their conduct
they called attention to the fact that I am the politically incorrect colour,
sex, and size. The effect was enervating. On their turf I felt as though, like
Dracula, they were sucking the very blood out of me.

Undoubtedly a few politicians have origins as humble as mine. But most of the ones I ran into seemed to act, after donning the political cloak, as if they had been gilded with a patina of privilege and money. Sadly, it seemed to me that having won their elections these formerly fawning candidates ceased acting as our wooers and became our bosses. Possibly this turn of affairs is both a byproduct of power and a prescription for their continued success in the democratic system. Perhaps they believed the old saying: act like a winner, because nobody votes for a loser.

We knew that our community could never survive a head-to-head confrontation on this battlefield. David with his slingshot needed only to hit Goliath's tragic flaw with devastating speed and accuracy, but we lacked even David's simple weapon. It seemed that our best plan, instead, was to pursue the strategy outlined by the sixteenth-century Japanese samurai Miyamoto Musashi. Musashi advised that when you are fighting a stronger opponent you should attack the enemy's strategic corners, thereby weakening him.[1] Musashi is perhaps best known in the west for *The Book of Five Rings,* a collection of his thoughts on life and survival. The title refers to the five elements: earth, wind, fire, water, and emptiness – Western philosophy has acknowledged only the first four of these. Musashi's book, written with Zen-like simplicity, reflected the military tactics of the period. In Japan, Musashi is an icon, one of the country's legendary figures comparable in stature to a samurai-cowboy. In North America, strangely enough, Musashi is also gaining notoriety because some members of the business community are studying his work to learn the "secrets" of Japan's economic success.

I speculate that a key to the NAJC's ultimate victory was the September 4, 1984, federal election. Suddenly an angry country unceremoniously turfed the Trudeau Liberals out of office and with the largest landslide in Canadian history voted in the Conservatives. Fortuitously for our cause, on his last day as leader of the opposition, in an angry exchange with Pierre Trudeau, Brian Mulroney publicly pledged to "compensate" Japanese Canadians if he were elected prime minister.

I theorize that if the Tories hadn't won, given our community's lack of political sophistication, the Liberals– longtime experts in ethnic control – would have sumi-wrestled us into submission long before we had had time to unrobe. Catching the NAJC offguard, the Liberals summarily would have signed a deal with the *shikataga-nai* faction. In the process our community would have lost its last chance at rebirth. The psychic lesions of the internment survivors would have continued to fester under the skin, and the rights of all Canadian minorities would have remained at risk.

On November 21, 1984, while the new government was setting up office, the NAJC released *Democracy Betrayed,* our case for reparations. Using documents that had only become public in the late 1970s, the brief proved that the government had interned twenty-two thousand Canadian residents against the advice of the RCMP and the military, both of which had reported that Japanese Canadians were no threat to Canada's security. The archival materials established that the government of the day was motivated by racism and political opportunism and that certain ministers, for their own ends, had systematically distorted information that they presented to cabinet.

It had long been a matter of public record that Prime Minister Mackenzie King, in response to questions in the House of Commons in 1945, had admitted that there was not a single documented act of espionage, sabotage, or fifth column activity committed by a Canadian citizen of Japanese ancestry or by a resident Japanese alien. At the same time, no mass property confiscations and sales, exclusions, or detentions had been ordered against Canadian citizens of German or Italian ancestry in any part of the country.

Initially the Tories appeared ignorant of "ethnic" issues. Largely untouched by multicultural politics, privately they must have wondered what the fuss was all about. Nonetheless, we found some members among their ranks who opposed bigotry and discrimination. One such person was the new Speaker of the House, British Columbian John Fraser, who was born in Japan.

In 1980, before the Special Joint Committee on the Constitution, Fraser said: "My father was a veteran of the First World War and had fought with Canadians of Japanese descent in the Canadian army in the trenches in France and whose memorial, as you will know, is still there in Stanley Park commemorating the Japanese Canadians who died for Canada in the First World War. He spoke out against the internment, not because he was not a loyal Canadian; not because he was not prepared to fight in the war that we were engaged in, but because ... what was being done to the sons and daughters of the comrades he fought with was contrary to the very British justice that we thought we were engaged in protecting in the fight against Nazism."[2]

The endorsation by other Conservatives, such as realtor John Bosley, can be explained in part by an opposition to government expropriation of private property. On May 10, 1984, while he was an opposition rookie backbencher, Bosley, along with Lynn MacDonald of the NDP, George Ehring of the Canadian Auto Workers, and Clarke MacDonald, the Moderator of the United Church, appeared at an NAJC press conference held in Toronto called to condemn Trudeau's handling of our injustice.

JACK MURTA 1984-85

Within months of assuming office, one of the more publicly heralded acts of the newly elected Tory government was to meet with the NAJC negotiators. In this respect at least, Manitoban Jack Murta, the Tory's first Minister of Multiculturalism, went one up on the Liberals. Aware that the thwarted Liberal proposal had been widely criticized for its lack of input from the Japanese Canadian community, Murta said he was prepared to sit down with the NAJC and negotiate a settlement. Not for him an old boys' agreement behind closed doors.

As a result of this promise, there was a flurry of winter meetings, as NAJCers flew into icy Winnipeg to meet with Murta and his officials. I remember one of these trips, when stepping off the plane, full of hope, I breathed deeply. Immediately I felt a strange sensation as the hair in my nostrils instantly froze: a harbinger of things to come. Initially we were heartened by Murta's openness. At the conclusion of our first meeting, on December 15, 1984, Murta and the NAJC issued a joint press release that stated that the parties had begun "a full and frank discussion" on a "timeframe for the process of negotiation; the amount and nature of compensation; the wording of the official acknowledgment of injustice and the steps to be taken to prevent the reoccurrence of such injustices." We were later dismayed to discover that Murta must have seriously misread the prime minister's marching orders. Within a month the minister had changed his tune. It quickly became obvious that there was not much, if any, room for negotiations. By the end of January 1985 Murta made what he said was the Mulroney government's "last best offer," which sounded suspiciously similar to the Liberal's offer under Trudeau: an apology and a $5-million or $6-million educational trust fund. A *Globe and Mail* editorial later opined, "How quickly atonement has turned to ultimatum."[3] Perhaps in response to editorial criticism and public pressure, Murta subsequently upped the government's offer to $10 million.

Somewhat shellshocked by the apparent about-face, the NAJC continued to reject all governmental threats to call a halt to further meetings and/or act unilaterally. Both sides were intransigent, deadlocked over the NAJC demand that the settlement include compensation to individuals that would bear some relationship to the losses suffered.

Nonetheless, we were astonished to learn six weeks into discussions with the new government that members of the *shikataga-nai* faction, community seniors as well as some Western members of the NAJC, had been invited to the House of Commons to witness a unilateral apology made by the Mulroney Government. NAJC president Art Miki was informed of this development by several unsuspecting NAJC council representatives who had been called. Immediately Miki got on the phone to members of the press to check out the story. The next day, on February 2, 1985, a *Globe and Mail* editorial criticized "an Alberta Tory member of Parliament" who "had offered to fly Japanese Canadian softliners to Ottawa to legitimize a settlement which the NAJC opposed." *The Globe and Mail* seized the occasion to take the government to task. The paper urged the Tories to "accept the NAJC demands for individual compensation and for an economic losses study to assess the dollar value" of the damages. The country's most influential paper further proposed that the "study's findings then serve as the basis of negotiations between Ottawa and the NAJC."[4] Unfortunately neither Murta nor his government seemed to have read the newspaper that day, or more likely they decided to ignore its unsolicited advice. However, there was satisfaction in having publicly caught the government with its pants down. I hope the P.M. read his backbenchers the Riot Act.

Murta, a federal M.P. since 1970 and certainly no political ingenue, tried a new tack. He began to pressure the NAJC to break up our redress package, to accept an apology that would "memorialize the Japanese Canadian experience" and to leave the negotiating of an acceptable financial settlement to a later date. This worried us. We on the NAJC strategy team knew that if the government apologized, the most traditional members of our community would feel obliged to let the matter drop. Playing by Japanese rules, they would feel that continuing to press for more would be unacceptably revengeful and demonstrate a lack of generosity on our part. We also feared that it would be strategically impossible to get the government back to the bargaining table once they had managed to relieve themselves of this albatross through a ceremonial "mea culpa."

The government continued to stall. As we were to learn, in 1985 there wasn't enough political ante in the issue for the Tories to consider a just settlement that would total in the hundreds of millions. It would take years before the political momentum would change. In 1985 it seemed that all the government wanted was to quickly sweep the controversy under the carpet. Backroom Tory strategists, misjudging the community, thought a simple apology to the survivors sweetened with an offer of $5 or $10 million would put the matter to rest. For years the Conservatives lived under the misapprehension that they could force us to accept what the Liberals had tried to bring about through secret backroom discussions.

OTTO JELINEK 1985-86

Within a year, like ducks in a shooting gallery, Murta went down and another cabinet minister popped up. This next one was Otto Jelinek, a 1962 Olympic ice skater and double-portfolio Minister of Fitness and Amateur Sport and Multiculturalism. Jelinek, then a twelve-year M.P. from Halton, was described by *Ottawa Citizen* journalist Roy MacGregor as "Rambo Jelinek." Unfortunately Jelinek did nothing to change this image and thoroughly managed to rankle those of us on the negotiation team. Attempting to ingratiate himself at an early encounter, he confidently divulged that he was on our wave length, because "like us he was a recent immigrant to Canada." Undaunted by our stony silence, Jelinek unwittingly emphasized what we all secretly feared: that as far as white Canadians are concerned, we would never be accepted – once a Jap, always a Jap.

Jelinek's background also concerned us. Several Eastern Europeans we had talked to had vigorously opposed the NAJC redress demands. Some of them regarded the injustices suffered by Japanese Canadians as simply the unfortunate side effects of war. They argued, "Look at us, we lost everything in the 1940s, including our homeland." Earnestly they pointed out that they would never see compensation from the Soviets for their miseries, so why should we expect that they pay for our misfortunes in Canada? We had trouble convincing them that a NAJC victory would make it more difficult for a future Canadian government to trample on their rights in Canada. Although we were concerned that Jelinek might also share these views, as it turned out we never had a serious enough discussion with him to find out exactly where he was coming from.

After several meetings Jelinek told reporters on January 28, 1986 that the NAJC was "dragging its feet." Knowing that Price Waterhouse would be releasing its report on the community's losses in the spring, Jelinek threatened that if the association didn't come up with a dollar figure "within one month," he would bypass us and deal with the "real survivors" (meaning the *shikataga-nai* faction) who were "not looking for individual compensation."[5]

The Minister of Fitness and Amateur Sports and Multiculturalism made me think again of Japan's samurai-cowboy icon Miyamoto Musashi, who like Jelinek was also concerned with winning battles. If Musashi had sat in on our meetings with Jelinek, he would have applauded the minister's strategy of using threats to induce fear of the unknown in his opponent. But Musashi would have also cautioned the minister that repeating the same ploy twice was a tactical error. In his "mountain and sea change" parable Musashi wrote that if your opponent expects mountains, give him the sea, and vice versa. Jelinek, ignorant of Musashi's advice, routinely tried to intimidate us with the same threat: do as I say or else.

Growing up in the tough working-class schoolyards of Hamilton had taught me how to discern between simple name-calling and more potentially explosive pushing and shoving matches. As a youngster you learned to quickly assess a bully's real intentions. Threats from cabinet ministers only strengthened the samurai knot that was forming in the pit of my stomach. Unlike the Brownie knots that I had practised as a child, a samurai knot tightens with each twist until it turns to stone.

From the beginning Jelinek refused to deal with the injustice done to our community. His response to our call for government acknowledgement of wrongdoing against innocent Japanese Canadians was a "general apology to Japanese, Jews, Ukrainians, Chinese and others who had suffered at the hands of the government." In response to our demand for meaningful compensation to the individuals affected, he proposed a $6-million educational foundation. To justify his refusal to discuss individual compensation, Jelinek portrayed the NAJC as greedy and himself as righteous. In December 1985 Jelinek issued a statement that Ottawa would not insult Japanese Canadians any further by offering money as compensation for the wartime sale of their homes, businesses and personal property. In the same vein, in March 1986 the minister went "as far as to say that 'real survivors' would not support such a claim" for individual compensation.[6] On May 14, 1986, in response to questions in the House from Liberal critic Sergio Marchi, Jelinek told Parliament, "In preparing the options for Cabinet the [wartime] losses were taken into consideration." But, he added, "There is more to the redress issue than financial matters. This is a moral matter."[7]

Several weeks later, NDP multiculturalism critic Ernie Epp accused Jelinek of being "out to sabotage the redress process" because he had used "a private telegram from five Japanese Canadian individuals in Vancouver to create the sense of divisions in the Japanese Canadian community."[8] Throughout the period, Jelinek refused to recognize the NAJC as the community's political representative and continued to meet with the compliant *shikataga-nai* faction. In response to his critics he justified his actions by saying that he had been holding meetings with "all interested groups."[9]

The Toronto Star, the country's largest circulation daily, had been openly disapproving of Jelinek's intrigues within the Japanese Canadian community and continued to push the government to negotiate a settlement with the NAJC. Irritated by the paper's editorials, Jelinek arranged to meet with the *Star's* editorial board. According to Don Sellar and Ken Adachi, who were members of the *Star's* editorial board, Jelinek's session with the paper's editors was "hot and heavy." Needless to say, Jelinek did not manage to convince the *Star* to change its position. In fact it appeared that Jelinek was out of step with Canadian opinion. In March 1986, Environics Research Group, as part of the regular Focus Canada-CROP poll, completed the first national survey of Canadian attitudes on Japanese Canadian redress. The results revealed that sixty-three per cent of Canadians favoured redress. Of those, seventy-one per cent stated that each individual who was treated unfairly should receive financial compensation.

DAVID CROMBIE 1986-88

By the late spring of 1986, rumours had been circulating that Jelinek was on his way out. The change was overdue. Commenting on the Conservative government's first major cabinet shuffle, a *Globe and Mail* editorial stated that Mulroney had "relieved" both parties (Jelinek and the NAJC) when Jelinek became "no longer responsible for arranging compensation for Canadians of Japanese ancestry interned during the Second War War."[10] In the days before the shuffle, members of the NAJC's strategy team had been collectively crossing our fingers: it seemed better times were ahead, because the oddsmakers were betting that the former Toronto mayor, the popular David Crombie, was slated for the job.

A year earlier, on a blistering winter's day, Roger Obata, Dr. Wes Fujiwara (popular president of the Toronto and North York chapters in 1984-86), and I had paid a visit to the newly elected Rosedale Tory M.P., David Crombie. Throughout the meeting in Crombie's Toronto constituency office, the new Member was friendly, affable and sympathetic. Crombie, who had been affectionately regarded as Toronto's "tiny perfect mayor," lived up to his advance publicity. At the end of our short get-together, the three of us came away feeling assured of his support. Crombie had just left a successful career in municipal politics, and soothsayers were predicting a bright, meteoric federal career for him. It was said that in exchange for a cabinet post, Crombie was expected to deliver Metro's traditionally Liberal ethnic vote on a silver platter to the Tories.

A year later we were to meet a slightly different man. Crombie was apparently feeling the weight of the "Japanese Canadian issue which had flattened his two predecessors" – in the words of *Ottawa Citizen* columnist Dan Turner.[11] The multiculturalism portfolio seemed to be gaining a reputation as a "meat grinder," in part because of our campaign for redress. Nonetheless, we still had high hopes that Toronto's "Red Tory" minister would be able to deliver where others had failed. When he finally did agree to meet with the NAJC, in November 1986, Crombie was as friendly and charming as ever. He repeatedly told us that the prime minister had put him on a "very short leash" and that the most he could offer at that time was $6 million, which at least, he said, was a million more than his predecessor had proposed. He seemed to be unaware that Jack Murta's final offer had been $10 million. [12]

A disappointed Art Miki told Crombie that we were not even in the same ballpark. Suddenly Crombie blew up. He had expected, I suppose, to be able to "reason" with us and convince us that the cupboard was bare. We were shocked at the outburst– unexpectedly this genial little leprechaun had turned red and vituperative. I couldn't help thinking about his well-known heart condition. Crombie even resorted to a Jelinek tactic, hinting that perhaps the government should be dealing with the soft-line *shikataga-nai* and not the NAJC. Then, with a sudden change of face, in hushed tones that dramatized its importance, Crombie informed the NAJC negotiators that he would be taking our issue to cabinet, but only after doing a series of cross-country consultations with various groups and individuals.

The minister for multiculturalism also announced that he would be presenting cabinet with a recommendation as to "process." Without knowing exactly what this meant, we maintained our hope that for the first time we had a minister who would advise his colleagues to abandon settlement by ultimatum and who could convince the cabinet to give him enough rope to try and settle the dispute through negotiation. Crombie promised that before he went to the cabinet he would get back to us. Crombie asked the NAJC to give him time to "study the issue and to become conversant with it." Given our experience with Jelinek, who had waltzed in blissfully ignorant of our history, this seemed to be a reasonable request.

Months passed. Our next meeting was held on a snowy afternoon in February 1987 in Crombie's Secretary of State office in midtown Toronto. We were heartened to discover that Crombie differed from his predecessors in two ways: He seemed convinced that the NAJC was the organizational representative of Japanese Canadians. No doubt by this time he had heard of the Toronto, Vancouver, and Lethbridge city councils' endorsations of the NAJC. Secondly, Crombie said that he would recommend to cabinet that community funds be controlled by the NAJC. In any case, generally amiable, Crombie lulled the NAJC into accepting his timetable. But by March 1987 even his charm was beginning to wear thin. Crombie had successfully mothballed our issue for nine months. Perhaps this tiny perfect minister was less than perfect after all.

Informed that Crombie was planning on submitting a redress proposal to cabinet in March 1987, NAJC members flew to Ottawa that month to lobby Speaker John Fraser, Dalton Camp (a consultant to the Mulroney government), Don Mazankowski (Deputy P.M.), Clifford Chadderton (a representative for the War Amps, who were representing the Hong Kong POWs), and multiculturalism critics Sergio Marchi (Liberal) and Ernie Epp (NDP).

Weeks afterwards Crombie wrote to Art Miki, outlining his long-awaited settlement package. He proposed only an acknowledgement of wrongdoing, a review of the War Measures Act, and a $12 million community fund. Disappointed, NAJC negotiators met with Crombie in May 1987 to plead with the minister to reconsider. Defending his refusal to support individual compensation, the minister suggested dividing the $12 million among the fourteen thousand survivors.

Two weeks later the NAJC Council rejected Crombie's offer. In what was to be one of our last meetings with the minister, in June 1987, Crombie again underscored the problems he faced. In his defence he said that he was constrained by the "small size of his footprint." He suggested that the solution lay in using accountants' and tax lawyers' tricks to miraculously make the $12 million blossom. Although we all agreed this was a good idea, we were sceptical that $12 million could become hundreds of millions of dollars even with the assistance of the country's most brilliant money magicians.

At this meeting Crombie did make some useful disclosures. He announced that as long as Japanese Canadian redress was considered an ethnic issue and not a justice problem, the government was not going to take it seriously. His aide, lawyer Ron Doering, a John Dean look-alike, said that the government's $12 million offer could be "substantially increased if Cabinet believed that they were paying the NAJC off to avoid a more costly law suit." Crombie reminded us that the government had other more pressing concerns and our grievance was close to the bottom of its priorities. He asserted that most Canadians were not interested in what had happened to us and that in the total scheme of things our experience was relatively insignificant. Needless to say, this didn't quite correspond with our view of the matter. We knew the issue was taking on more importance in the country – in fact, I had once been told that Queen Elizabeth had asked Crombie what he was doing to resolve the Japanese Canadian redress problem.

On one level Crombie seemed sympathetic to our cause. He said that to win we would need to make the government re-examine its shopping list, and that a law suit or a settlement in the United States could cause an about-face. But then, years later, we were surprised to learn from Gerry Weiner that despite all his expressed interest, Crombie had never taken the Japanese Canadian redress issue to cabinet for discussion.

By June 1, 1987, Crombie, angered by the NAJC's refusal to accept his unilateral offer, called off all further meetings with us. Towards the end of July 1987 Crombie sent Art Miki a letter that made one thing clear: although the minister had changed, the message was still the same. The only offer on the table remained the $12 million proposal for a foundation. Crombie wrote that the government had reached the end of its patience; like all his forerunners he was giving us a "take it or leave it" ultimatum. At the time it seemed like Crombie had adeptly outmanoeuvred us. He, like all the other ministers, had put the NAJC on the defensive. We began to think that it was time for us to turn the tables and take the offensive.

GERRY WEINER 1988

After our experience with Crombie I was beginning to doubt the NAJC's decision to abandon the legal route in favour of the political road. Having personally placed my hopes on Crombie, I was devastated by our impasse. The minister's ability to charmingly put us off and to keep us waiting for over a year had weakened our organizing drive. Waking up to this reality, the NAJC began to consider those alternative plans that involved taking our case more publicly to the people and possibly to the courts.

Silently, like a duck sliding into the water, in the spring of 1988 a fourth minister mechanically appeared in the shooting gallery. Our initial meeting with Gerry Weiner confirmed the grapevine gossip: that here was a man prepared to listen. We were also impressed with Weiner's assistant, Dennison Moore, a likeable South-East Asian and born political fixer. During a pause in a meeting Moore would take one of us aside to get an informal, impromptu reading of the situation, in exchange for his own interpretations of the government's pulse. This was a cultural practice common to our community, and a useful one. After all, what is said during a session is often secondary to what happens before and after it.

In our last meeting with Weiner – the final August 1988 negotiations – the minister reassured us that there was no disagreement over the wording of the acknowledgement of government wrongdoing. We had been told years earlier, in fact, that much of the apology reflected the prime minister's thinking on the subject. Weiner said the government shared our concern over civil rights protections, and he believed that the new Emergency Powers Act would provide sufficient legal guarantees to prevent a reoccurrence of our history. He reminded us that as a Jewish Canadian mindful of the Holocaust he also wanted to prevent the same kinds of things from happening again.

Although Weiner was no doubt instructed by the P.M. to strike a deal with the NAJC, my memories of him are positive. I am not surprised, however, that associates who work with refugees know a different politician; and I feel betrayed by the government's failure to honour its final commitment to us. Now, years after the signing of our agreement the government is reneging on the establishment of the Canadian Race Relations Foundation. By the terms of our 1988 settlement, a foundation would be set up to fight racism. To this end, $12 million was "donated" by the Japanese Canadian community to be matched by an equal contribution from the government. The Act establishing the foundation has never been proclaimed and with a change of government could be lost.

ED BROADBENT

In earlier years, if there was any political loyalty in the Japanese Canadian community, it was to the Co-operative Commonwealth Federation (CCF). From the time of its founding in 1932, the CCF was consistently our only champion, sometimes to the party's own detriment. In the 1935 elections, for example, the Liberals campaigned that "a vote for any CCF candidate is a vote to give the Chinamen and the Japanese the same voting right as you have." In those days, with friends so few and far between, Japanese Canadians developed a feeling of obligation to the handful of CCFers who had fought for us.

Not surprisingly, then, in the 1980s we also felt some loyalty with the

CCF's offspring, the New Democratic Party. Whenever we went to Ottawa to lobby the politicians, I always felt most comfortable in Ed Broadbent's office. The surroundings – filled with natural light, plants, and Canadian aboriginal artifacts– were welcoming. As you might expect with a former academic, his shelves and tabletops were spilling over with papers and books.

After being greeted warmly by Broadbent and the NDP's multiculturalism critic, Ernie Epp, the NAJC strategy team would squish down into the two sofas and spill onto chairs hastily dragged in from surrounding rooms. Broadbent in person seemed to be the same Ed we knew from television, approachable and decent. On each one of our regular visits we got a sympathetic hearing and a commitment of support. The friendliness of those meetings stood in sharp contrast to the reception that we had received from the other two parties. For political babes-in-the-woods like ourselves, those other audiences were unnerving experiences.

Broadbent's affinity to our cause was partly political and partly personal, because his first wife, Yvonne Yamaoka, was a Japanese Canadian. Yvonne's father, Seitaro Yamaoka, had worked as a youth on whaling ships off the Pacific coast of British Columbia and later sold Christmas trees from a downtown Vancouver corner. Eventually he managed to set up and operate his own saw mill, Powell Lumber. He developed a process for reusing rejected lumber that made him a small fortune. Before the outbreak of the Second World War he was exporting a million dollars' worth of lumber to Japan a year. In 1942 the Yamaokas were forced to relocate to the B.C interior. Over the next seven years, as if in a nightmare come true, the family lost the accumulation of a lifetime's hard work and saw their civil liberties, their personal dignity, and their community destroyed. By 1950 the Yamaokas had moved again, this time to Toronto, where Broadbent's former father-in-law, at the age of sixty-five, began stoking coal on barges that dredged Lake Ontario.

In her book on Ed Broadbent, journalist Judy Steed wrote that the experiences of his first wife's family "had a huge impact" on him. He was outraged by Trudeau's refusal to apologize to or compensate Japanese Canadians. Broadbent said that Trudeau "refused to recognize the unique nature of the Japanese Canadians' circumstance. They never did anything wrong and they lost everything."[13]

It wasn't until recently that I learned that Yvonne and her family had spent the war years in the same relocation centre as my family. I have a picture taken in 1943 of my parents, my four-year-old brother Rick, and my two-year-old sister Pat, tightly clutching her teddy bear, all surrounded by some forty-odd members of the McGillivray Falls self-supporting community. A young Yvonne Yamaoka and her older sister, Setsu, are also in this photograph. Setsu had just graduated from university and was asked by the McGillivray Falls parents to set up a school for the interned youngsters. She was my brother Rick's first teacher.

JOHN TURNER

The leader of the opposition, John Turner, represented a curious contrast to both Ed Broadbent and the Conservatives. In those days Turner, speaking only for himself because his party was on the point of disintegration throughout this period, would deliver thinly veiled advice that the NAJC needed to be "reasonable" if we wanted to continue to rely on the support of the Liberals.

Our meetings with Turner were held in his gloomy suite in the Parliament buildings. That very office, complete with granite columns, had formerly been the workplace of Mackenzie King. Glancing around this huge and draughty mausoleum where King had once held his cabinet meetings, my eyes were mesmerized by a large wooden desk in the corner. Perhaps, I thought, it had been around that very table that King and company had planned our ruination. Turner's remarkable Paul Newman-blue eyes and stiff anglo persona only confirmed my fears that we had wandered onto the wrong stage set. I wondered, with our yellow faces, how did we get past the receptionist? My feelings of discomfort were intensified by the tensions in the room. The caucus members present at those meetings coldly referred to Turner as "The Leader" and never by name – and even Turner tended to speak of himself in the third person. "The Leader thinks ..." he would say. In spite of the reassuring presence of Sergio Marchi, the Liberals' multiculturalism critic and a staunch redress supporter, a sense of unreality hung over those meetings. I always felt that the room was haunted by the ghost of Mackenzie King.

An interesting sidebar came to light while I was researching this book. Apparently, in 1968 Secretary of State Judy LaMarsh had handed Turner, who was the new Minister of Justice, an old and tattered grievance. Eighty-seven year old Torazo Iwasaki had sued the government for

$1.5 million dollars, claiming that decades before the Custodian of Enemy Property had acted improperly in selling his land on B.C.'s Salt-spring Island. Turner's familiarity with secret government files went back over twenty years, but he never once let on.

BRIAN MULRONEY

To this day, Brian Mulroney remains a mysterious figure to me. The press continually reported statements by the prime minister indicating that he was prepared to get together with the NAJC and that his "door was open at all times."[14] Yet why did he ignore Art Miki's letters and phone calls?

Once, in desperation, we were referred to two Ottawa lobbyists, highly placed within the Tory party apparatus, who promised for a fee to arrange a meeting with Mulroney. They had a sliding scale of services that they could provide for outsiders like ourselves. I found the idea curiously offensive. During the late 1970s, when Toronto was cracking down on body rub parlours, I had defended some masseurs who also had a graduated price list. My clients were always found guilty and fined for their activities. We declined the lobbyists' tantalizing offers to get us into the Centre Block's inner sanctum. Art Miki continued to write and to leave telephone messages with the prime minister's secretaries.

Unexpectedly, one Saturday shortly after the September 22, 1988 announcement, Mulroney did try to telephone Art Miki at his home in Winnipeg. I had read that for relaxation the prime minister spends leisure time calling his buddies across the country on his private watts line. For some unknown reason his secretary had dialed Art. Keiko, Art's wife, answered the phone. She believed it was a friend playing a joke on her husband because it was a well-known fact in the community that Mulroney never returned any of Art's calls. As it happened Art was out at a friend's cottage. Keiko, finally convinced that the call truly was from the P.M.'s office, gave a forwarding telephone number. Apparently Mulroney phoned Art there, but this time it was Art who wasn't in. Later, when Art tried to return the P.M.'s phone call, it was business as usual. Actually the first and only time that any of us ever spoke with Mulroney was on September 22, 1988, the date of the public signing in Ottawa.

I like to think that the prime minister, with sporting grace, had called Art to congratulate the NAJC on our surprising victory. Certainly when we started our campaign for justice in 1984, no oddsmaker would have placed money on this ragtag group of determined amateurs. Still, even in the bleakest times the NAJC refused to give up. We felt the onerous obligation to regain not only our own personal family's honour, but also that of our community.

Armed only with our history and with *nebari* (stubbornness), we managed to turn a moral embarrassment into a sword. From the experience of the issei and nisei we learned that judges were immune to our brand of *nebari* and moral injustice. Fortunately, we found that politicians are less likely to be as indifferent.

IN 1942 CANADA SENT A LOT OF KIDS TO CAMP

You were born in Canada. Your parents were Canadian citizens. But that didn't stop the government.

Family property was seized and sold for a fraction of its worth. Your father was assigned to forced labour. You and your mother were transported to flimsy tarpaper shacks in the middle of nowhere, and left to cope with —30° winters.

Because you were a Canadian of Japanese descent, this would be your life for the next four years.

This, you discovered, was Canadian "democracy" at work.

WAS IT NECESSARY?

Were these drastic measures implemented against some 22,000 men, women and children necessary for national security?

The RCMP produced strong evidence to the contrary, but were overruled by the government.

Two tragic years later, this same government would publicly admit that no act of subversion by a single Japanese Canadian had ever been found before or during the war.

THE WRONG REMAINS

After the war.they were left with little but the feeble utterances of succeeding governments. And for 41 years nothing's changed.

The present government proposes a unilateral quick fix in the name of "Multiculturalism" that does nothing to redress the real injuries suffered by these Canadians of Japanese ancestry.

It is time to right the wrong once and for all. Time, in the eyes of the world, to redress this long-standing failure of Canadian democracy itself.

WHAT YOU CAN DO

Join us in petitioning the Government of Canada to: (1) negotiate solely with the National Association of Japanese Canadians, the community's elected voice for over 38 years, (2) formally acknowledge government wrongs during and after WW II, (3) establish a just formula for . compensation, and (4) insure through appropriate legislation that no future government can similarly mistreat another minority.

RIGHT THE WRONG
Support Japanese Canadian Redress

X

Please sign this ad and send it to:
**The Canadian Council of Churches
40 St. Clair Ave. East
Toronto, Ont.   M4T 1M9**
It will accompany our formal petition to Ottawa.
Toronto Ad Hoc Committee for Japanese Canadian Redress.

A tax-deductible donation toward the cost of this ad would also be greatly appreciated. Please make cheque payable to "Canadian Council of Churches (Redress)".

Advertisement that kicked off a campaign launched by the Ad Hoc Committee for Japanese Canadian Redress, March 6, 1986.

8 | Taking It to the People

> When authority in any form bullies a man unfairly all other men are guilty; for it is their tacit assent that allows the authority to commit the abuse. If they withdrew their consent, authority would collapse.

> – Pierre Trudeau

OUR COMMUNITY'S WHITE, or *hakujin*, supporters often remarked with a mixture of awe and astonishment about the NAJC's "stubbornness." Because of our refusal to quit, ours was a moral issue that just wouldn't go away. Our allies, accustomed to negotiations where the bottom line is a bargainable monetary figure, were mystified by our demand that the settlement be both just and honourable. Once the community had made the decision to reclaim its dignity, there was no turning back. There was little leeway. With honour, how can half measures be acceptable?

Perhaps we gained strength from so-called eastern relativism. A journalist once asked Chairman Mao what he thought were the results of the French revolution of 1789. Mao, rubbing his chin thoughtfully, apparently replied, "It's too early to know." Although we Japanese Canadians do not share Mao-Tse Tung's historical vision, we nonetheless took a longer view than our opponents. After one particularly futile negotiation session with Otto Jelinek, the sansei on the NAJC strategy team jokingly declared that perhaps we would have to pass the job of redressing the injustices done to our community to our offspring, the *yonsei*, (fourth generation). Possibly, we thought, our children would have more success with the next generation of Canadians. Since our community wasn't planning on folding up its tents and disappearing into the night, we were prepared to wait.

Largely because we lacked clout, redress in Canada followed a completely different tack than in the United States. Although Japanese Canadians were finally granted the franchise in 1949, we remain a community without representation in the Canadian power elite. Unlike the situation in the United States, there are no Japanese Canadian judges, senators, or politicians to influence the state's apparatus. Out of necessity ours was a grassroots movement that piggy-backed on the success of our American cousins. In the United States, the issue of reparations for Japanese Americans had become a political question, and there the bulk of the community's efforts was directed to getting the Civil Liberties Act through Congress and signed by the president. Here we lacked the power to meet with Mulroney, let alone lobby him to pass a Japanese Canadian Redress bill.

The NAJC strategists determined that Canadian politicians would only sit up and take notice if we made our issue a matter of concern for all Canadians. Internally, this approach meant that we had to develop political expertise within our community. On the organizational front we needed to constantly disseminate information and diffuse opposition both inside and outside the community. Ultimate victory required the winning of media support to help build public support.

In many ways the media was the key to our success. Supporters such as pollster Jim Matsui advised the NAJC to develop a media strategy to get the story out. Because ours was a largely unknown history, we determined that first Canadians needed to be told what had happened during the 1940s and then led to understand why forty years later our community was seeking redress.

On comparing our two strategies, my American Japanese colleagues remarked upon both the quantity and degree of positive coverage we received in Canada. But in our initial efforts, in the 1983-85 period, we found to our dismay that the press preferred to reduce our item to yet another ho-hum ethnic squabble between the "radicals," meaning the NAJC, and the "moderates," the *shikataga-nai*. To be fair, there were indeed different opinions within the community, each with its own organizational representatives. However, by portraying our issue as a petty feud between two warring factions and by concentrating on the divisions within our community, the press managed to both confuse Canadians in general and further deepen the rift between Japanese Canadians. More seriously, by not telling our wartime history and by failing to identify the real combatants– Japanese Canadians versus the government – the media's approach allowed government politicians to ignore our claim.

Recognizing that this coverage was a major political roadblock as well as a community irritant, the NAJC spent considerable time meeting with journalists, trying to convince them of our legitimacy and of the importance of the issue. On the former, we were undoubtedly helped by the decision of Toronto City Council to recognize the NAJC as the representative of the Toronto Japanese Canadian community.

One of our first and perhaps most important meetings took place in January 1985 when Roger Obata, Don Rosenbloom, and I met with *The Globe and Mail* editorial staff. After removing our winter snowboots in the hall, we were ushered into the packed office of *The Globe's* editor, Norman Webster, and motioned to sit on a sofa. We found ourselves facing a row of seated, white, middle-aged men. No one smiled, offered us tea, or exchanged small talk. Webster unceremoniously began to pepper us with questions. The others joined in during the discussions, and a few of them silently scribbled down some notes. Webster's questions were direct, astute, and at times hostile. Never before – and never since – have we faced such thoughtful scrutiny outside of our own community. When the audience was over, Webster stood up. We shook his hand and thanked the nameless others for their time.

Before we could change our minds about what now seemed to be the demonstrated futility of trying to influence the press, we hopped into a taxi and headed over for a meeting with *The Toronto Star* editorial board. Based on our first experience we assumed that we would again face a firing squad of journalists armed with stiletto pens and poker faces. Instead we met only with cheerful Don Sellar, a member of the *Star's* editorial board. Sellar and the *Star* editors, it turned out, were already sympathetic to the NAJC and the issue of redress. Sellar said he had especially wanted to get together with us, so that in the future he would be able to put faces to names.

Afterwards, rehashing the afternoon, Roger Obata and I were completely perplexed by our ordeal at *The Globe and Mail*. I was even more surprised the next morning when I opened the paper and read a strong editorial endorsing the principle of a negotiated settlement with the NAJC.

For the following four years both *The Globe and Mail* and *The Toronto Star* continued to support our claim and sympathetically cover the issue. Roger Obata and I made it a priority to maintain contact with both papers, and after redress was won the NAJC publicly acknowledged the role that the Toronto press had played in our success. Indeed, the NAJC's press strategy had paid off so well that by 1987 most journalists routinely treated our controversy as a justice and civil rights battle between the Japanese Canadian community and the government, and not as a factional dispute.

Our relationship with the city's third newspaper, *The Toronto Sun*, known for its "tits and ass" pinups and right-wing editorials, was mercurial. Although the *Sun* opposed the goal of individual compensation, it backed our claim in part because as a matter of principle it was hostile to property expropriations without reimbursement. Somewhat predictably, a 1984 *Sun* editorial had attacked the Trudeau Liberals' refusal to compensate as an indication of their socialistic tendencies.

When *The Toronto Sun* continued over a period of time to cover redress as a community spat, Roger Obata and I decided to meet with its publisher, Paul Godfrey, and its editor-in-chief, John Downing. Godfrey, a former politician accustomed to dealing with delegations of irate citizens, had the manner of a friendly pacifier. Both men listened to our arguments and, not surprisingly, promised nothing. Although later we did note changes in the *Sun*'s treatment of the subject, the shift was probably unrelated to our visit. News coverage tended to dry up, although over the years several of the *Sun*'s iconoclast maverick columnists, such as Peter Worthington and Dalton Camp, began to urge the prime minister to honour his word to Japanese Canadians.

Roger Obata and I went through much the same exercise with local television news directors and reporters. On TV our story was routinely limited to sporadic ten-minute mini-histories on public affairs programs or to thirty-second interviews whenever some event in our continuing drama was deemed to be newsworthy. Strangely, only the writers of situation comedies or soap operas presume that television viewers have recall facilities. News programs make no such assumptions. Is it the case that all those minds using computers, fax machines, and teletype can no longer comprehend cause and effect?

The only external organized and vocal opponents to redress were WWII veterans, some of whom still viewed Japanese Canadians as enemy aliens. On May 16, 1985, the Ontario Command of the Royal Canadian Legion formally voted against reparations to Japanese Canadians. According to Roy Cleator, provincial secretary, only two out of thirteen hundred delegates present at the meeting spoke out against the motion. Amazingly, the Ontario Command compared the internment of the Japanese in Canada to the imprisonment of Canadian soldiers in Japan. As *The Lethbridge Herald* commented, the Ontario Command's motion "clearly shows that the Ontario Legion cannot tell the difference between Canadian civilians and Canadian soldiers in battle. The Japanese Canadians interned in Canada were civilians. Most of them held Canadian citizenship. It was their own government which took arbitrary action against them because of their race."[1]

Fortunately, the Ontario Command of the Royal Canadian Legion stood more or less alone in its approach to redress. The secretary of the Dominion Command said it was "highly unlikely" that it would "sanction a motion of this type."[2] In April 1985, Ben Bianchini, president of the Army, Navy and Air Force Veterans in Canada, an organization with some fifty thousand members, stated that he believed that Japanese Canadians should receive some compensation for their losses. "They were staunch Canadians when the war broke out and had no intention of being treacherous," he said. But, somewhat diplomatically, Bianchini said he did not know enough about the Ontario Command to offer any criticism of its position.[3]

In the United States, the Japanese Americans received the endorsations of the American Legion and the Veterans of Foreign Wars. During the war, Japanese Americans had been recruited into Japanese American battalions, which distinguished themselves valiantly. Some thirty-three thousand Japanese Americans served in the war. Most renowned for their bravery were the eighteen thousand men who served in the 442nd battalion, one of the most decorated combat teams. During seven major campaigns, this regiment suffered 9,486 casualties, including 600 killed.

The slogan of Japanese Americans soldiers had been "Go for broke," a kamikaze attitude that won them the respect and admiration of the other soldiers.[4] (In fact the Japanese American redress bill HR442, eventually signed on August 10, 1988, by President Reagan, was named in honour of the Japanese American soldiers of the 442.)

After the war, Japanese Americans soldiers continued to stay involved in their veterans' associations. In typical American style, once these vets had decided to support redress they went all out. They launched a nation-wide educational travelling photo display, prepared brochures, gave talks to local service clubs, and sold "Go for broke" buttons. When the Japanese Americans vets appeared en masse at their local and national veterans' conventions to ask for the support of their fellows, they generally got it – though often not without some initial argument or prejudice. Wisely, the endorsations mouthed motherhood principles that most Americans would find difficult to oppose. The motions commended the Japanese American battalions for their bravery and condemned unconstitutional government actions against loyal citizens.

The situation in Canada was completely different. We were hindered in our campaign by our government's racist actions in the 1940s. Japanese Canadians had been refused entry into the armed forces until the last days of the war, when the British began to recruit Japanese Canadians out of the need for translators who understood Japanese. At that point, shamed, the Canadians also started to accept recruits of Japanese ancestry. As a result the number of Canadian Japanese vets was small and they had not had the same opportunities to display their patriotism and valour as the Americans. In the end the national body of the Canadian Legion refused to become publicly involved in the issue. The NAJC was able to convince the Canadian veterans' organizations not to lobby against us, although we never did obtain their public support.

Early on the NAJC realized that without the support of a broad coalition of Canadians our cause was dead in the water. At the time, as the person on the strategy team "assigned" to build non-Japanese Canadian support in Toronto, I began by placing a few phone calls to Toronto friends in the Jewish, Italian, Chinese, Black, and South-East Asian communities. They encouraged me to come and make presentations to meetings of their national or provincial executives.

In the beginning we found it difficult to speak to strangers about "our shame." Even today most Japanese Canadians are unable to discuss this central event in their lives with their children. Initially the NAJC was embarrassed that the first time our community approached our neighbours it was to ask for assistance. We felt anxious going hat in hand to strangers appealing for their help. In our culture, a request so delivered would be tantamount to an order and extremely difficult to refuse. Because the people we were approaching were all *gaijin*, or foreigners, the uncertainty of how they would respond weighed like a heavy stone in our stomachs. But from the beginning of the campaign we found a diverse collection of allies. Not surprisingly, our strongest support came from other ethnic and visible minority organizations, as well as from the churches, the trade union movement, and civil libertarians.

On February 9, 1985, Roger Obata and I made our first presentation to the National Association of Italian Canadians (NAIC). The group wasn't totally unfamiliar with our wartime situation, because some members of their community had been subject to curfew and incarceration. NAIC became one of the first organizations to support our cause, and the sympathetic endorsement that we received from the Italian Canadians was replicated time and again. The networks established in Toronto were developed further by members of the NAJC strategy team in Vancouver, Winnipeg, and Montreal. Through those contacts, adopting an aboriginal saying, we became more accustomed to "walking in the moccasins of others."

Given all the possibilities that existed for miscommunication, it is a wonder that we were able to successfully convey our burden. No doubt we were helped in this by the sad fact that ours was a timeless and universally understood tale. Again and again I went away from these meetings impressed by the calibre of the men and women seated around the tables of the ethnic associations. These individuals form the cream of the country's leaders – yet they are largely shut out from mainstream politics, despite being as talented and bright as any of the so highly esteemed cabinet ministers I have encountered.

Our campaign was helped by the release in 1984 of a government report on visible minorities in Canada, *Equality Now*, which made several recommendations related specifically to Japanese Canadians. They were that: "The Parliament of Canada should officially acknowledge the mistreatment accorded to the Japanese in Canada during and after

World War II and the Government should undertake negotiations to redress these wrongs.... Justice Canada should review the War Measures Act with a view to proposing safeguards necessary to prevent a recurrence of the kind of mistreatment suffered by the Japanese in Canada during and after World War II."[5] In 1984, after discussions with the Toronto Mayor's Committee, Toronto City Council, always sensitive to ethnic issues, became the first level of government to urge Mulroney to reach a negotiated settlement with the NAJC. In the following year Vancouver's and Lethbridge's City Council followed suit.

Although coalition ethnic politics is still in its infancy in Canada, we identified other minority groups that we thought would support our cause. In Toronto we worked not only with the National Congress of Italian Canadians, but also with the National Jewish Congress, the Chinese Canadian National Congress, and the National Association of Canadians with Origins in India. On our behalf these organizations sent telegrams of support to the prime minister and lobbied within the Canadian Ethnocultural Council (CEC), an ethnic umbrella organization representing thirty-five communities. They spoke out at public rallies that we organized on redress. Art Miki was elected to the CEC executive and effectively won the support of some minorities who had initial reservations about endorsing us.

One of the first groups to come to our defence was the Mennonite Central Committee of Canada (MCCC). Without any prompting on our part, on October 30th, 1984, the MCCC officially apologized to Japanese Canadians because some members of the B.C. Mennonite community had "benefited from the wrongful sale of Japanese Canadian lands in the Fraser Valley." One of the initiators of this apology was John Redekop, a professor at Wilfrid Laurier University in Waterloo and a member of the MCCC. Redekop, who was a young boy when the events happened, recalled wartime dinner-table conversations that revolved around the treatment of Japanese Canadians. His parents were familiar with discrimination – they had immigrated to a Saskatchewan farm from the Ukraine because of persecution from the Russians and the Ukrainians – and their religious community held firm on its belief that racial bigotry was incompatible with Christian values. In 1944 many Mennonites, including Redekop's family, had moved to larger, more prosperous farms in the Fraser Valley. He remembers that "Jap farms" dotted the area.

In one of his regular columns in the *Mennonite Brethren Herald,* Redekop made a "modest proposal": "Quite a few Mennonites bought farms which really belonged to the evicted Japanese Canadian owners. I have walked on many of those farms. Already in the late 1940's my conscience bothered me, even though our farm did not belong to the category in question. With governments continuing to drag their feet we must finally act, even if only symbolically. Let us, through the MCCC, pay at least a token of $10,000 to the NAJC. That would, at least, be a start."[6]

At an MCCC Board meeting in September 1984, Redekop suggested that although "Mennonites had not been responsible for the injustice, yet some Mennonites had benefitted from it." He encouraged "the children of the benefactors to come to terms with the children of the victims." At that meeting the members of the MCCC executive personally established a $10,000 fund. Interest from the fund would initially go towards providing scholarships for needy students of Japanese Canadian ancestry.

Other old friends who returned to defend the Japanese Canadians in the 1980s were former members of the Co-operative Committee on Japanese Canadians (CCJC), which had been set up in the 1940s. This time, led by Cyril Powles, a retired Anglican clergyman and a professor of divinity at the University of Toronto, the CCJC reconstituted itself into the Ad Hoc Committee for Japanese Canadian Redress. Other initial members of the Ad Hoc Committee were Michael Creal, Frank Cunningham, Ben Fiber, and Alice and Dan Heap.

Cyril Powles, a charming and genial man, is extremely knowledgable about Japanese culture and history and fluent in the language. Now over seventy years ago, Cyril was born in a Japanese mountain resort town, famous as the initial meeting place of the current Emperor and his commoner wife. Cyril's parents were missionaries stationed in Japan and Cyril spent his first fifteen years there, until the outbreak of war forced the family to return to Canada. In the 1940s the backbone of the CCJC had been Japanophiles and Canadian missionaries, who, like Cyril Powles's parents, were knowledgeable about the country and people. When they returned to Canada they were shocked at the virulent hatred of Japanese Canadians, and they began to work through the churches to counteract the prejudice and ignorance of white Canadians. Cyril's father, Percy, was head of the Montreal Co-operative Committee.

During the war the Canadian government had asked Percy Powles to help its war effort by interpreting Japanese maps. Powles's response was that he wouldn't endanger his neutrality, because if he did so he could never return to Japan.

At war's end, young Cyril Powles was hired by the CCJC to organize reception committees across the country to assist Japanese Canadian families being released from B.C.'s internment camps. To dispel racist myths Cyril helped to prepare pamphlets that outlined facts and fiction about Canada's "enemy aliens." Years later, his blue eyes twinkling, Cyril still recalls having to avoid blows from irate white Canadians in centres such as Lethbridge and Vancouver.

True to his word, in 1947 Cyril's father, at the age of sixty, went back to Japan to continue his church work. In 1949 Cyril and his wife Marjorie also returned, and they remained there until 1970. The family's ties to the country continue through one of Cyril's sons who is married to a Japanese woman and lives in Japan.

Initially contacted by my husband to assist in developing a coalition of supporters, Powles immediately telephoned other old Japanese Canadian community allies. One of them was Ernie Best, a conscientious objector during WWII who had been sent to teach Japanese Canadian high school students in the Tashme, B.C., internment camp. At Tashme, Best met Helen McWilliams, the daughter of missionaries who had been stationed in Japan. When Japanese Canadians were moved to the B.C. interior, Helen's father, "Mac" McWilliams, had chosen to follow his Japanese Canadian congregation from Richmond to Tashme. Best ended up marrying Helen and after the war they moved to Japan to continue their work.

In the early days of the struggle, the Anglican and United churches threw their support behind the NAJC's campaign for justice. Anglican Archbishop Michael Peers culled through old church resolutions passed in the 1944-48 period that had opposed the government's mistreatment of Japanese Canadians. He traced the Anglican Church's concern for justice for Japanese Canadians back four decades. Acting in concert with the NAJC, the Toronto Ad Hoc Committee directed its activities towards the general public. The Committee began holding open forums, initiating letter writing campaigns, and building a national support group. The drive began in force in March 1986 with a *Globe and Mail* advertisement initially sponsored by the Canadian Council of Churches, which offered its charitable number to the cause so that income tax receipts could be given to donors. The ad featured a grainy photo of Japanese Canadian children being loaded into army trucks under the headline, "In 1942, Canada sent a lot of kids to camp." Its public letter, addressed to Brian Mulroney and signed by hundreds of groups and personages, called for a negotiated settlement with the NAJC. In response to the ad, thousands of Canadians wrote in from across the country, enclosing donations. Cyril Powles, who had participated in many similar campaigns over the years, remarked that for the first time in his life it felt good to be involved in an economically profitable venture. For Cyril the positive response was a good sign of how the climate in the country had changed since the 1940s.

There were inevitably some places where we failed to win backing. Just as the NAJC lacked highly placed allies in the Tory party, we similarly had no friends in the country's business elite. Although we were not surprised, we were regretful that none of the Chambers of Commerce or members of the Canadian business establishment came to our defence.

Personally more disappointing was an indifferent response from the organized women's movement. From our experience in the mid-1980s I sadly concluded that Canadian feminists were not ready, at that time, to view racism as a feminist issue. Although perhaps sympathetic to our cause, the NAJC never received any recognition or endorsation from the organized women's movement. In 1946, through the churches and the YWCA, women had been centrally involved in the campaign against the Mackenzie King government's plan to exile and repatriate the Japanese Canadian community to Japan. Somehow, in the forty years that had elapsed since those days, we had lost the support of the organized women's movement.

Aware of this tension, in an address that I made at a public rally in Toronto on International Women's Day in 1985, I argued that the women's movement was becoming narrowly self-interested and adopting an almost biological approach in deciding the issues to concern themselves with. I reminded them that during the 1960s and 1970s half of the faces of the white southern bigots who were screaming and protesting against desegregation nightly on our television sets were women. I asked them to accept the fight against racism as a women's issue. Sadly, although my speech met with strong applause, in the three years that followed there was no further communication from the organized women's movement. This is not to say, however, that women did not support our cause. For instance, in June 1985, delegates from thirty-three countries at an international women's peace conference in Halifax passed my motion affirming support for the NAJC's campaign to redress the injustices perpetrated by the federal government during and after World War II. The motion stated, "In particular, we urge the Canadian Federal Government to make meaningful redress to the Japanese Canadian community."

With Canadian feminists now beginning to accept "Canadian women of colour" into their midst, signs are hopeful for the 1990s. This will surely mean a continuing, and painful, examination of Canadian racism. Currently the smoke from this debate is being fanned within the Canadian arts community as well. As an observer, I can only cheer on those who are lobbying the Canadian arts establishment to pry itself away from the white-anglo stranglehold. From the sidelines I can hear the huff and puff of indignation and denial.

In October 1987 the Ad Hoc Committee and the Toronto Chapter of the NAJC organized a public forum in Toronto. The leaders of twenty national ethnocultural organizations representing some nine million Canadians of neither English nor French derivation joined the Toronto support committee and, for the first time publicly, urged the government to negotiate a settlement with the NAJC. At the meeting, Vancouver leader Roy Miki announced the transformation of the largely Toronto-based Ad Hoc Committee into a national coalition. He announced that a "Freedom Day" rally would be held in Ottawa in April 1988.

As scheduled, on April 14, 1988, after months of planning, the National Coalition and the NAJC organized a placard-carrying march on Parliament Hill. The work was co-ordinated by Reverend David Murata, a Toronto United Church minister, assisted by dozens of members of the Toronto, Hamilton, and Montreal chapters of the NAJC, the Canadian Ethnocultural Council, Dalton Camp (the former national president of the Progressive Conservative Party), and MPs Ernie Epp (NDP), Sergio Marchi (Liberal), and Alan Redway and David Kilgour (PC).

The rally's purpose was to shame the government into action. Nine months had gone by since the July 11, 1987 meeting when David Crombie had broken off talks with the NAJC. Since then, angered by the NAJC's rejection of their $12 million ultimatum, negotiations had been deadlocked. Meanwhile we were aware that the Civil Liberties Act, Bill HR442 compensating Japanese Americans had already been passed by the House of Representatives and was before the Senate. We felt the need to turn on the heat. The demonstration, designed both as a media event and a community morale booster, culminated in a theatrical rally in the House of Commons. NAJC senior citizens, politicians, and the press attended a program packed with fiery speeches and music. Escorted by parliamentary guards, we delivered four large mail sacks stuffed with fourteen thousand yellow postcards demanding a negotiated settlement to the Prime Minister's office. The postcards were the work of Japanese Canadians who had gone house to house and got Canadians from coast to coast to support us. A more unusual gimmick that caught the attention of the media was the distribution of twenty thousand artfully designed redress napkins that publicized the event throughout Ottawa. With the help of several MPs, the napkins were smuggled into the Members dining room on Parliament Hill.

By April 1988 it seemed that our movement's long years of discussions had become part of a healing process. I saw the psychological transformation within my own family. Initially my sister and mother argued against my redress involvement. They claimed that the Mackenzie King government's actions had been for our own good. My sister, like many others, still maintains that the community's internment and uprooting were on balance beneficial because the experience destroyed once and for all times the Japantown ghetto and forced us to assimilate. But as the years passed my mother and brother had become financial and active supporters of the NAJC. At seventy-five years of age, and despite the decades she had spent advising me of the dangers of such activity, my mother attended the April demonstration – her first ever – carrying a placard like so many others. For some, like my reticent brother, the campaign was a reassuring eye-opener. He remarked with surprise that white Hamiltonians signed the postcards with less hesitation than did Japanese Canadians.

Now, many years into our campaign, relatives who had avoided discussing the issue had finally started to ask me how things were going. They even began to attend NAJC-sponsored meetings. As organizer

David Murata pointed out by April 1988 the National Coalition included a who's who of the country's best-known personalities, organizations, and unions. Among the signators were over two hundred organizations and thousands of individuals. Towards the end of the campaign Murata's office was being deluged with letters, and the support embraced all the important sectors of the nation, with the notable exception of the business community.

Slowly the tide of public opinion had turned in support of Japanese Canadians. The ubiquitous public opinion polls offered a tangible sign of this growing support. In 1987, forty-two per cent of those questioned by Gallup approved compensation. A month after the announcement of a redress settlement in Canada, on October 27, 1988, another Gallup poll revealed that fifty-three per cent were aware of the Japanese Canadian compensation package and approved of the government's actions. The highest regional support was in British Columbia, where fifty-nine per cent of the respondents favoured redress. The prairies had the lowest approval rate, with forty-seven per cent backing reparations. The trend to higher acceptance continued: a year after the settlement, an Environics poll indicated that seventy-six per cent approved of the government's apology and fifty-two per cent supported the financial compensation package. The NAJC had done its homework and laid a strong factual and political groundwork for its claim. For Japanese Canadians, and for Canadians in general, redress was long past due.

9 | Glass Ball Reflections

An alliance for freedom,
taken with the idea of freedom:
it all becomes clear
in the small mirror of sincerity.
Yet while we lament, asking
why our insignificant selves
were oppressed,
the rain still falls
heavily on the people.

Genzaburo Ohashi, 1892 quoted from *Kabasan jiken*[1]

GENZABURO OHASHI, an uneducated farmer, wrote his poem in 1892, shortly before he died in his prison cell. Ohashi had been jailed for his participation in a peasants' uprising against the Japanese government. He was a member of the Freedom party that had attempted through armed revolt, to overthrow an oppressive leadership in September 1884. The rebellion, called the Kabasan incident, occurred along Japan's western coast, north of Tokyo.[2]

My ancestors, like almost all the Japanese in Canada, descended from peasants steeped in a history that validated revolt in the face of extreme injustice. During the Tokugawa period (1590-1867), there had been some 6,889 recorded peasant insurrections – averaging about twenty-five a year for almost three hundred years.[3] According to some scholars, the tradition of revolt in Japan was an inherent part of traditional Confucianism, which validated the use of armed force against greedy rulers and heartless governments.

A common saying that expressed the cruel elitist attitudes of the period was, "Peasants are like sesame seeds – the more you squeeze them, the more they produce".[4] Under Japanese feudalism peasants had only the right to subsistence and any surplus they produced was immediately confiscated by landowners and the government. The injustice of this system, particularly in years of famine, drought, or other natural disasters, would result in peasant delegations requesting local authorities to forgo that year's taxes. If that appeal fell on indifferent ears, violent insurgency was the only other available recourse. This philosophy and tradition, like the *Yamato* legend, were part of the folklore that the Japanese brought to Canada. Thousands of miles away and decades later, we sansei, using the weapons of the twentieth century, also fought to rectify a wrong perpetrated against us by malevolent forces. Armed not with swords, bombs, and pitch forks but with opinion polls, newspaper editorials and placard-waving demonstrators followed by television cameras, we were able to arm-wrestle the government into acquiescence.

In the months after the September 1988 settlement, once the enormity of our victory had sunk in, I found myself asking three questions: why did it happen, what does it all mean, and was it too little, too late? After years of seeing the government alternately bully or ignore us, I was puzzled why, in the final months of their first term of office, the Tories had changed their tune, seemingly overnight. What had caused them to raise their "last and final offer" from $12 million to a figure closer to $400 million? Possibly we will never know what brought about this sudden shift in policy. Perhaps we will have to wait until the shroud of the thirty-year Official Secrets Act protecting Canadian and U.S. cabinet documents is lifted to know the real answer.

Until very recently, I had believed that Mulroney was the key to unlocking this puzzle. The question that I turned over in my mind was what motivated and moved our prime minister into action? Paramount in my speculations was his well-publicized following of the opinion polls and his concern about how history would remember him. The members of the NAJC negotiation team had been told that Mulroney was nervous about an important address he was scheduled to make to the United Nations in late September 1988. Perhaps that explains why, fifteen days after President Reagan had signed the $1.25 billion Civil Liberties Act compensating Americans of Japanese ancestry, we in Canada were signing an agreement with Mulroney's cabinet trouble-shooters. Apparently he didn't want to be embarrassed by the precedent set by his friend and guiding star.

Certainly, a key to our victory had to be the U.S. settlement, which had happened only days before. Strangely enough, the White House's opposition to Japanese American redress had been a matter of record for years. Reagan's advisers had said that even if the Japanese American redress bills successfully made their way through the House of Representatives and the Senate, they would counsel Reagan to exercise his presidential veto to block passage of the legislation as a matter of fiscal responsibility. Perhaps the better question to ask, then, is why did Reagan ignore the advice?

Timing was also on our side. Political analysts, interpreting the public opinion polls, pronounced that the ethnic minorities were getting restless and that Canadians did not trust the prime minister. Newspaper columnists wrote that Mulroney was getting spooked by his declining popularity and that with the additional pressure of an upcoming federal election he was jittery.

Finally, there was the constant pressure and presence of the NAJC. We were proving to be a small but irritating thorn stuck in the government's side. Undoubtedly Mulroney's sources had informed him that we were planning strategies on how to put redress on the upcoming election agenda, right alongside the dominant issue of free trade. It had been embarrassing enough that Japanese Canadian pickets had crashed the economic summit meetings held in Toronto in the summer of 1988. The leaders of the world's seven economic powers had to pass through a gauntlet of Japanese Canadians distributing literature. Conservative journalist Peter Worthington wrote in the *Financial Post* about the motley crew of Japanese Canadians dressed "in robes banging a drum complaining that there has never been redress to Japanese Canadians interned during WWII."[5] Astonishingly Worthington urged the prime minister to honour his promise to Japanese Canadians. Behind closed doors, Mulroney must have grumbled how "they" just wouldn't give up and go away. Japanese Canadian redress had proved itself to be a nagging moral issue that wouldn't die.

In my mind, at least initially, these were the major factors that had convinced Mulroney to make good on his widely publicized 1984 pre-election promise to compensate Japanese Canadians. However, one morning a year after our settlement, while semi-consciously eating my bowl of bran cereal and reading *The Globe and Mail*, I chanced to see an interesting explanation for the Alberta Lubicon Indian land-claim settlement.

I had watched that drama played out on my television screen months before. Nightly, the story had unfolded like a morality play. At issue was the ownership and control of thousands of acres along the Peace River in northwestern Alberta. The Lubicon Band was contesting the provincial and federal government's rights to the land. Dressed only in a thin nylon windbreaker, with a peaked cap atop his black pony-tail, the young Lubicon chief Bernard Ominayak had said that his small band of Cree were desperate. Fifty years of federal and provincial government stalling on their land-claim demands had placed his people with their backs against the wall. Armed only with angry words and a baseball bat, he swore that they were prepared to die if necessary.

I was impressed by Ominayak's passionate determination and guilted by the comparison between his plight and my comfortable Toronto life. He struck a raw nerve. I was not fighting for my home, even though the bank owns it in more ways than I care to think of. Anyway, I would be the first to acknowledge that my moral dilemmas are more mundane. I was embarrassed and awed by the Crees' fierce desperation. Within days the media recorded that Donald Getty, the former football quarterback and now Alberta Tory premier, had undergone a quick change of heart. Perhaps, I thought, his office had been deluged with phone calls from all over the country giving him hell. Or alternatively, giving the premier the benefit of the doubt, I wondered if he too had been moved to tears by the Cree's sorry plight.

Riding his white charger, Getty had gone to Ottawa to champion the Lubicon's cause with his federal colleagues. Suddenly television cameras documented the slight Ominayak, still dressed in his cap and windbreaker, signing an accord with the suited, beefy Getty. I settled back into my happy cocoon. "Ah so, democracy at work. Canada isn't such a bad place to live in," I thought to myself. This sweet delusion lasted until an article by Andrew Nikiforuk and Ed Struzik appeared in *The Globe and Mail's Report on Business Magazine*. Apparently, in the fall of 1987 Daishowa, Japan's second-largest pulp and paper manufacturer, with global sales of $3 billion, had negotiated a twenty-year lease with the Alberta government for twenty-four thousand square kilometres on the Peace River. Part of this land was the subject of the longstanding Lubicon land claim. In 1988 Lubicon band members picketed Daishowa's offices in Vancouver. Embarrassed by the publicity, Daishowa's general manager Koichi Kitigawa flew to Edmonton to speak with Getty, "sparking rumours that Daishowa was threatening to cancel the mill if the Premier didn't settle the real estate dispute...(Upon settling the claim) Getty, who has no previous record of aboriginal advocacy, insists that Kitigawa never hinted at pulling out."[6]

This astounding revelation got me thinking. Suspiciously, the Canadian and U.S. Japanese settlements stand out in the 1980s as two of the few human rights victories in a bleak decade dominated by right-wing business-oriented governments. I had known since 1983 that the NAJC's U.S. counterpart, the Japanese American Citizens' League (JACL), had been meeting with Japanese premier Nakasone and his senior officials. The visits were not publicized in the United States, but the JACL made sure that President Reagan and the White House Foreign Office were kept informed of the subject matter of the discussions. I had always wondered why in the grand scheme of things someone as important as Nakasone would bother to schedule meetings with the JACL, which is a relatively insignificant U.S. volunteer ethnic association.

In the spring of 1985, Roy Miki of Vancouver and I, as members of the NAJC's strategy team, were sent to San Francisco to establish links with the various U.S. redress movement leaders. There I met Ron Wakabayashi, the JACL's executive director. Ron was in the midst of organizing the JACL's delegation to meet with Nakasone, members of his cabinet, and leading Japanese business officials. The JACL urged us to establish relations with the Japanese government because they felt this connection would put additional pressure on the White House and could also influence our negotiations with the Canadian government. The JACL was concerned about our inability to move the Canadian government from its low $6-million offer. They were fearful that such a picayune settlement north of the forty-ninth parallel would seriously undermine their own $2-billion demand for compensation.

Although Ron's arguments for establishing contact with the Japanese were persuasive, in the end the NAJC decided against following in the

JACL's footsteps. National Council was afraid that such a tactic could backfire. They worried that if we brought the Japanese government into the picture Canadians might not see redress as a Canadian issue of Canadian citizenship and Canadian justice.

Perhaps NAJC Council was correct to steer clear of the Japanese. Years later in my search for research funds for this book, I approached ten of the largest Japanese multinational corporations in Canada about donating a portable computer and a tape recorder. It was a small request, perhaps at most amounting to a tax write-off of a few thousand dollars, but I was turned down by them all. What puzzled me was not their refusal but their total inability to see – even in the strictest of business terms – that they had a direct interest in Canadians knowing our history and in Canada being a more tolerant society of racially unbigoted consumers. I am afraid of their insensitivity because, unlike them, I do not have the option of pulling up stakes and jetting over the Pacific when crosses are burnt on my front lawn. With our common ancestoral yellow skin, I must suffer from the backlash caused by their actions in my country.

As a Canadian, just as disturbing to me has been their mercenary single-mindedness. Yet I speculate that perhaps it was this very self-interest that started a nervous tremour in Tokyo about the wartime precedent whereby in Canada the property of persons of Japanese ancestry had been seized and sold without compensation. Perhaps the Japanese corporations wanted assurances that the billions they were investing in North America would be secure from government expropriation.

Robert Brown, vice-chairman of the accounting firm Price Waterhouse, matter-of-factly stated that "fifty billion dollars could leave the Canadian market within a few days if even a few Japanese investors turned sour."[7] Reaffirming Japan's awesome economic clout, William Purves, chairman of the Hong Kong and Shanghai Banking corporation, remarked in an address to international financiers that "even the rumour of an investment decision by major Japanese financial institutions is enough to move the securities markets of the world. Japanese direct investments are transforming the industrial structures of North America, Europe and Asia."[8] Perhaps it was this fear that kept our tight-fisted finance minister Michael Wilson from opposing the spending of $400 million; perhaps it was seen as the necessary price for retaining in Canada the billions of dollars held by the Japanese giants. This is, of course, total conjecture, but having been naively caught out on the Lubicon native land-claim settlement, I am prepared to entertain a more sophisticated explanation involving Machiavellian international intrigue.

In 1989, to test out my theories, I returned to Los Angeles and San Francisco to interview the former leaders of the Japanese American Citizen's League. Years had passed since I had been to California and seen my Japanese American counterparts. I arranged to meet sansei Ron Wakabayashi, the former head of the JACL, on Cranshaw Boulevard in downtown L.A. at the Asian American Drug Treatment Centre. Over a decade earlier Ron had helped establish the hostel because of a series of sansei drug overdoses. In 1988 he left the JACL after eight years as its executive director. He had presided over the JACL throughout the important redress years and had gone on the 1983 and 1985 JACL delegations to Japan. I believed that if any American Japanese had ideas as to why the American Congress had passed the compensation bill, why Reagan hadn't exercised his presidential veto, and why the Japanese were interested in this issue, Ron might.

According to Ron, American Japanese won redress because of the happy convergence of the U.S. bicentennial celebrations, the upcoming federal elections, and Reagan's anxieties about how history would record his tenure. Ron opined that the Civil Liberties Act of 1988 was passed by Congress because of "hardwork, lucky timing, and karma". He attributed the hard work to Japanese American stubbornness and the effective lobbying of American Japanese senators and congressmen. In particular he singled out Democratic senator Spark Matsunaga, who had represented his home state of Hawaii for twenty-six years. Matsunaga, a highly decorated WWII veteran, had lobbied each senator personally. Sadly, Matsunaga died in 1991 at the age of seventy-three in a Toronto cancer treatment clinic.

Ron supported my view that White House concerns about Japan had played a role. In Ron's opinion, Reagan viewed Japan as an economic partner and, as an ideological free trader, was opposed to the Democratic party's Japan bashing. The Japanese, for their part, had a strong interest in the treatment of American Japanese. The issue of redress was regularly covered in the Japanese press. Ron noted that throughout the U.S. redress campaign Japan and its economy always got more press coverage than the issue of American Japanese redress, despite Japanese efforts to stay out of the limelight. As far as Ron was concerned this indicated both the importance of Japan to the U.S. economy and his community's relative insignificance.

Ron credits Frank Sato for his role in influencing Reagan. Sato, president of the JACL in 1984-86, had been a high-ranking and respected civil servant under both the Carter and Reagan administrations, holding the position of Inspector General (an independently appointed auditor) for the Department of Veterans Administration. As JACL president Sato led the organization's delegations to meet with Japanese premier Nakasone and had briefed Reagan's advisers in the White House on the subject of the bilateral talks. Interestingly, both Sato and John Tateishi, the director of the JACL's redress program from 1981 to 1986, downplayed Japanese business influence on the White House. Tateishi disagreed with Ron and me that Congress had concerns about scaring away Japanese investment. Tateishi believed that Congress felt that "Redress was an American issue that needed to be settled on American soil."

After years of observing the president, Sato had an explanation for Reagan's support for the legislation. He said that Reagan only vetoed a bill for two reasons: if it carried a high dollar cost (and in the U.S. government's scheme of things $1.5 billion was not a big ticket item) or if it undermined some precept that Reagan felt strongly about. Although the Reagan administration had been labelled as anti-civil rights, Sato believes that Reagan was "okay on human and civil rights". He explained Reagan's opposition to school busing as not being primarily racist but as running counter to another principle that Reagan valued more strongly, namely the preservation of neighbourhoods and local schools.

Initially, according to Ron Wakabayashi, the Japanese were not concerned about the Japanese American redress campaign. However, the Japanese quickly became more interested when it appeared that American Japanese might be successful in influencing Congress. Sensitive to the rising anti-Japanese sentiment sweeping the States and fearful of Congress's increasing trade protectionism, Japanese government officials and top business leaders hoped that American Japanese could help them understand the inner workings of the American mind and political system. Through a series of meetings with the JACL, the Nakasone Japanese were educated about white racism and became supporters of American redress. Just as in 1907, when Japan's military might had resulted in a

"Gentleman's Agreement" with Britain whereby Japanese Canadians received better treatment than other non-white immigrants at the time, perhaps in 1988 Japan's economic power had helped to fashion both settlements. How else to explain why in this country, Japanese Canadians went to the head of the line, rather than much larger and more powerful lobby groups such as the aboriginal, Black, Chinese, Italian, and Ukrainian Canadian communities?

More thought-provoking, perhaps, is trying to determine what it all means. I believe that there are at least five major repercussions of our settlement: historical, moral, legal, political, and personal.

I had hoped that the historical implication of the government's acknowledgement of wrong-doing would immediately result in the rewriting of Canadian history, whereby the blame would be placed where it seems appropriate, namely on the shoulders of the government of the day. This has, unfortunately, not been the case. I am frustrated, for instance, when I hear respected Canadian historian Jack Granatstein continue to argue that a possible Japanese Canadian fifth-column activity was a justification for the government's internment of an entire community and the seizure and sale of their property. In his book *Mutual Hostages*, published in 1990, two years after the Canadian government publicly acknowledged wrongdoing, Granatstein persists in using this defence.

My animosity towards Granatstein's work goes back several years. In an article published in *Saturday Night* magazine in 1987, Granatstein supported the Mackenzie King government's actions against Japanese Canadians in the 1940s. Worried about the impact that such a charge could have on Canadian readers and on our negotiations, a consortium of supporters approached the eminent Canadian historian Ramsay Cook to request that he set the record straight. Cook wrote a letter to David Crombie, the Minister of Multiculturalism, stating, "The account of the events of those years given in Professor Granatstein's article is unfounded and the conclusions drawn in the final paragraph of the article misleading".[9] Cook charged Granatstein with offering "no concrete evidence" of traiterous activity and of misleadingly suggesting that fifth column activity directed by the Japanese consul in Vancouver continued after the war had begun. According to Cook, this activity was clearly impossible "since the Consulate was closed and the consul sent packing."

As Granatstein had noted in his article, in August of 1944 Prime Minister Mackenzie King stated in the House of Commons that "no person of the Japanese race born in Canada has been charged with any act of disloyalty or sabotage during the years of the war." Professor Cook concludes his letter by saying that "Granatstein's research does nothing to alter this judgement." Unfortunately, Cook allowed writer Joy Kogawa to print his attack on Granatstein's scholarship only in the Japanese Canadian press, so although it was professionally quite devastating, Cook's condemnation did not receive wide public attention.

A second impact of the settlement – which the government itself has emphasized – has come in the form of its moral implications for the country. Certainly the very fact of the settlement affirms a humane ethic of compassion and a concern for justice. Mulroney stressed in his speech to the House of Commons on September 22nd, 1988, the need to "face up to the past" in order to meet the "challenges of the future". Mulroney's words and actions stand in sharp contrast to Pierre Trudeau's parting words. In response to questioning in the House on his last day as prime minister, Trudeau refused to apologize to Japanese Canadian survivors on the grounds that the internments and property confiscations had been legitimately taken by elected representatives. Angrily he retorted, "I cannot rewrite history. It is our purpose to be just in our time and that is what we have done in bringing in the Charter of Rights."

Trudeau's renowned steel-trap mind had no doubt been clogged by the debris of dead small animals. Lamentably I regard Trudeau as a magician who dazzled us for over a decade with his social justice rhetoric that in the end was largely smoke and mirrors. In the heated parliamentary exchange between Trudeau and Mulroney, I noted three Trudeau fallacies.[10]

First fallacy: that wartime actions can be justified simply because they are taken by democratically elected politicians. The court at Nuremberg looking into the Nazi regime's atrocities said that no government can hide under a cloak of self-serving laws to justify its own immoral and unjust acts.

Second fallacy: that rectifying past injustices is rewriting history. Yet this is what Canada attempted to do when the Nova Scotia Royal Commission determined that Nova Scotia Mic Mac Indian Donald Marshall should receive $270,000 for having spent eleven years of his life behind bars for a murder he did not commit. History was not rewritten in awarding compensation to Marshall, but an injustice was imperfectly rectified.

Third fallacy: that the Charter of Rights and Freedoms necessarily protects other Canadians from the Japanese Canadian experience. In 1942, 120,000 American Japanese were also forcibly removed from their homes on the west coast and "relocated" to "exclusion centres" in the name of national security. Yet the United States, unlike Canada at the time, had a constitution that made inalienable rights of citizenship, property, and freedom of movement sacrosanct. Nonetheless, even the presence of a constitution did not protect American Japanese from the racist hysteria of the times.

In Canada all our precious and easily mouthed liberties, set out in the Charter of Rights and Freedoms can be eliminated or severely tailored to suit the fashion of the times. Section one of the Charter states that our rights are limited by "reasonable limits prescribed by law" that can be "justified in a free and democratic society." During the 1940s, with a war going on, the government's actions would probably have met that test.

An important third result of the Japanese Canadian settlement is the legal precedent that it sets. Afraid of opening the floodgates to other aggrieved groups, the prime minister was quick to point out that the government was simply "righting a moral wrong." He and all the government lawyers have been careful to maintain that the government was in no way admitting legal liability for the actions taken during the 1940s.[11] They hoped to limit the Japanese Canadian precedent to the very particular facts of our case. And if what happened in the United States is any indication, the government has little cause to fear. In 1987 the National Committee for Japanese American Redress, after finally exhausting all its legal appeals, was forced to drop its lawsuit against the U.S. government.

I still maintain, however, that the Japanese Canadian agreement sets an important legal precedent. Not because we would have lost in the courts but because we won a $400-million settlement from a budget-cutting government in spite of a weak legal case. Consequently such an astonishing precedent can only strengthen existing Canadian legal rights, our yet largely untested constitutional charter liberties, and the still unformed body of class action law.

The fourth consequence is political. That one of the smallest minorities in the country was able to make a forty-year-old wrong a national concern speaks well of the decency of Canadians. Building on this sense of fairness, Japanese Canadians were able to create a national coalition comprised of most of the country's ethnic groups, churches, unions, and human rights associations. These ordinary Canadians felt an urgency to protect the rights of minorities.

Although some of them had suffered discrimination in their pasts, for most the support for Japanese Canadians was an altruistic gesture. Their image of Canada as a just amd humane country had been shattered. In 1964, at the official opening of the Japanese Canadian Cultural Centre in Toronto, Prime Minister Lester Pearson referred to the internment and evacuation of Japanese Canadians as a "black mark against Canada's traditional fairness and devotion to principles of human rights." Many Canadians wanted this black mark erased. To their detriment, the majority of Canada's minorities, Japanese Canadians included, are self-absorbed in their own affairs and concerns. Coalition politics is something new. Encouraged to fight amongst themselves for ethnic dollars and token appointments to boards and commissions, minorities have often devoted their political skills to infighting and not to taking on the actual political powerbrokers.

Through the building of a grassroots national movement, my community discovered the benefits of coalition politics. We non-anglo, non-francophone "ethnics" account for over thirty-five per cent of the country's population, but by no means do we wield one-third of the power. During the fall 1988 elections an "ethnic" umbrella organization was formed to raise the profile of minority issues. Roger Obata was the Japanese Canadian representative on a working group that included seven "ethnic" associations. Gradually we are learning that the potential for flexing our political muscle is limited only by our inability to see beyond our own backyards.

The last consequence of the settlements – and the most difficult for me to evaluate – is the effects of the outcome on my community and my family. Some effects are straighforward. When my mother received her $21,000 payment, I asked her what she intended to do with it. She replied, "I think I'll put into a five-year Guaranteed Investment Certificate." Her response typified a life that had weathered the economic depression of the 1930s, the loss of everything in the 1940s, and then the decades of poverty as the family tried to get back on its feet.

Now when I travel across the country I notice that the nisei are more willing to speak to me about their past. Often it is with great difficulty, shame, and anger that the pent-up sorrows come spilling out, but at least now they are able to give voice to those feelings. The NAJC helped to educate the community about the true facts of the 1940s, thus ending years of speculation and rumour. Psychologically, for some who preferred to believe that the Canadian government had acted paternalistically, the act of facing the mounting evidence of their government's cold-hearted racism was difficult to bear.

Certainly redress was a form of recuperation and of exorcism. At a public community meeting in 1984 David Suzuki said, "As an adult, I ended up in psychoanalysis and was shocked to discover that virtually every psychological problem I had traced right back to the evacuation." Before redress the community similarly seemed to be in a state of psychosis. But by bringing a shameful past into the open and, more importantly, by demanding and fighting for its rights, the community became engaged in an important healing process. This healing had begun early on, as part of the redress campaign, and the energy created by the unleashing of those pent-up emotions was channelled into marches, signing petitions, organizing meetings, and attending rallies. For those who had taken the "cure," for the first time in their lives redress made them feel proud of being Japanese Canadian. As Joy Kogawa has expressed it, finally we could feel comfortable in our skin. We had gone through the nine stages of a rape victim that Margaret Atwood and others have detailed, and we emerged from the experience not just battered, but also wiser and stronger.

That strength is something I feel daily. It wells inside me whenever I hear of an injustice. It makes me feel that through the building of public support, anything is possible. I believe that if my community survives, it will be due in part to the struggle we went through and the exhilaration of our subsequent victory. I hypothesize that a group is empowered by having been successfully involved in a democratic struggle. If our campaign for redress was our community's last flicker before our total assimilation, it is not a bad act upon which the final curtain is drawn.

Personally, redress has opened a Pandora's box for me. I am experiencing the novel phenomenon of having Japanese Canadian friends and, for want of a less hackneyed phrase, of searching for my roots. Before I got involved in the redress movement I had concerned myself very little with the Japanese Canadian "community." Now I argue with my Japanese Canadian friends about whether or not we have a community and, if so, whether it will continue to exist despite our propensity to marry outside of our own people. With an intermarriage rate among sansei that hovers around ninety per cent and with a *gosei*, or fifth generation, now being born with only twenty-five per cent Japanese ancestry, I have to question what it means to be a Japanese Canadian. Blocked from access to that proud and rich culture because I no longer share the religion and, more importantly, the language of my ancestors, I seem to have more in common with white Canadians than with my distant relatives in Japan whose facial features resemble my own.

Robin Ostow, a sociologist friend, argues against racial categories and adds that religions can be adopted and language and therefore culture can be relearned. She points out that Hebrew was a dead language until forty years ago. Although I might agree intellectually, I wonder about my unborn *gosei* grandchild who would be only one-quarter Japanese and no longer share a physical resemblance with me; but if she took the effort to learn, she could speak Japanese. Would she qualify as a Japanese Canadian and could she and her siblings form a Japanese Canadian community? Frankly, I doubt whether she would even be encouraged to undertake the momentous task of learning the language that the *gaijin* call the "devil's tongue" because of its subtlety of nuances.

Perhaps it is racist to harbour such ideas. After all, what does it matter if a small group of Japanese Canadians assimilates and disappears? There are millions of Japanese back in the land of the rising sun. And certainly race mixing is a better alternative to racial segregation. If North America's visible minorities follow in our footsteps, wouldn't Martin Luther King's dream become a reality?

At the end of the day I have to agree with David Suzuki that redress may have been "too little, too late." But I differ from Suzuki because I believe that redress was better than nothing. At least the settlement may stand as an impediment against other Canadians having to go through our experience. I like to reassure myself that regardless of whatever tawdry machinations might in the end be revealed to explain the U.S. and

Canadian settlements, they did establish powerful precedents limiting the power of the state and protecting minority rights. The Canadian sleep can be less troubled and our country is all the better for having carried out this gesture.

When I measure what we achieved against what we had set as our initial goals, I am sorely disappointed. The NAJC had such noble dreams. At one point we aspired to forever rid the land of the War Measures Act and its replacement, the son of the WMA, now called the Emergency Procedures Act. We hoped to establish within the Constitution not only the right of equality for all Canada's minorities but also protection from our past. This was the legacy we wanted to be remembered for. I feel sorrow that we do not leave behind a treasure of such strength and worth. Perhaps if we had been more in number or had waged a more valiant struggle I would not feel such shame when I see the words of the final Order-in-Council dealing with my people. That document, I fear, is neither a shield nor a sword, but a bookkeeper's account. Pay them their $21,000, even though we, the Canadian government, did nothing legally wrong. It is hard to feel pride when I reread Order-in-Council P.C. 1988-89/2552, either as a Japanese Canadian or as a Canadian. In the end we are not heroes. My expectations exceed our abilities.

Over a century ago we landed on these shores, brought by the warm waters of the "Kuroshio," or Black Current, which travels a perpetual circle from Japan south to the Pacific islands, and then up along North America's west coast and back again. Transplanted adventurous peasants from a feudal island, we helped to clear the forests, to harvest the seas, and to develop a virgin country. In those days, Japanese fishermen attached glass balls the shape of grapefruits or small watermelons to their fishing nets to keep them afloat. Thousands of these balls freed themselves and have been drifting westward on the waves of the Kuroshio, eventually to be washed up on Canada's shores. Buffeted by the sea and the winds, the glass balls are a beautiful opaque bluish green colour. For some, they are simply the flotsam and jetsam tossed onto the beach, for others they are exotic objects of interest, collector's items.

Carried here by the warm waters of the Kuroshio we were also pummelled by the sea and the winds, and over the years our skins have been sandpapered by the hostilities we have endured. Rubbed raw, rubbed smooth. Perhaps we are Canada's living glass balls.

❀ | Epilogue

> The emergence of political power of aboriginal peoples is said to be the fulfilment of an ancient prophecy. We have been warned that either we stand with those who love the Earth, or we perish.
>
> Joy Kogawa (1991)

IT IS THE FERVENT wish of my community's moral leaders that Japanese Canadians learn to reach out and help others. Energized by the redress "victory" that we'd worked so long to win, the NAJC Council drew up an ambitious agenda: to rebuild our devastated community and give support to our aboriginal kin. One of the first acts of National Council was to set up a Japanese Canadian-Native Task Force, to investigate how we could best lend support to the most badly treated people in our country. Empowered by our own recent success, Japanese Canadians felt the need to share our good fortune with others.

At first some within my community questioned our decision to take up another group's cause for justice. Still, on various levels, Japanese Canadians feel bonds of kinship with the people of the First Nations, perhaps because at base we come from the same racial stock and there's a sense that together we've shared a history of discrimination in North America. Anthropologists speculate that Canada's aboriginal peoples migrated from Mongolia across the Bering Strait to North America. Having returned recently from living in northwestern China, near Mongolia, I am willing to attest to the many ties that bind us Japanese Canadians and the First Nations to the Tang people. When I used to mention this theory to Native friends, invariably they laughed and replied that the facts were reversed. "We fooled you all," they said, "those footprints in the snow. We had our moccasins on backwards."

Our meetings with the aboriginal community started with potlucks held at the Native Friendship Centre in downtown Toronto: plates of sushi beside pots of venison stew. The centre is next door to a Native seniors home, so invariably the elders came for supper as well. It became a regular community event. Over a period of a year the Japanese Canadian-Native Task Force evolved into the Earth Spirit Festival that took place at Toronto's Harbourfront in the summer of 1991. In the early days there were some feelings of discomfort on both sides. Through being together we learned to look beneath the surface into each other's hearts. We had much in common.

Over a period of two years, members of the Toronto Japanese Canadian and aboriginal communities voluntarily contributed thousands of hours of time to put on the three-day festival that highlighted their two cultures and a mutual concern for the environment. The event was an unqualified success. Organizers estimate that a hundred thousand people visited the craft, dance, theatre, music, and food tents. My *hakujin* friends, commenting on the "good vibes" remarked that they could not remember ever having seen groups of First Nations people at Toronto's Harbourfront. I was told by Native people that it was the first time that they had felt welcome at a city event.

After our smash hit, feelings were high about running the event again. Members of the Festival board seriously considered which direction our Japanese Canadian association with aboriginal peoples should take. It was decided that, at least for the time being, the Earth Spirit Festival would remain a Toronto-centred event and that each year another ethnic group would join with First Nations people to host the celebration. As a first possibility we approached the Chinese Canadian community. We hope that after ten years' time strong links between aboriginal peoples and Toronto's other minorities will be forged through the experience of having worked and shared experiences together.

✿

Two years after the settlement, my husband Frank Cunningham and I were living in Amsterdam, Holland. Somewhat unexpectedly, just before we were slated to return home, Japanese academics invited Frank to give a series of lectures in December 1990 in Yokohama, Kyoto, and Hiroshima. I decided to tag along. This would be my second voyage to the "sunrise isles," and twenty years since my last visit. Buried memories, like air bubbles, started to resurface slowly.

A plan began to formulate. I would make a pilgrimage to my ancestors' villages, which are within striking distance of Kyoto and Hiroshima. I knew my father, now deceased ten years, would have been pleased by the idea and that my mother would be relieved at the news. Both had been filled with feelings of guilt for never having visited their parents' graves. With this small gesture, I would fulfil two generations of filial obligations. For a month, letters crisscrossed the Atlantic as my family in Canada tried to obtain current Japanese addresses from my grandmother's faded and torn album. Next followed a flurry of correspondence to Japan as I wrote to sundry friends and associates for help in contacting my long-lost family. I was successful in locating a cousin of my father's in the town of Hikone, near Kyoto, but I kept striking out on the maternal side. It seemed that vague postal directions had worked well enough in my grandparents time, but by 1990 my mail was coming back with "address insufficient" stamped across the front. By chance, Dr. Jinzaburo Takagi, a nuclear physicist and the leader of Japan's anti-nuclear movement, was passing through Amsterdam. When he learned of my dilemma he kindly offered to locate my mother's kin. As well, Kaz Ide, president of the Japanese Canadian Association in Japan, formed as a result of our redress settlement, volunteered his members to act as guides and interpreters.

A month later I was in Japan. While Frank was lecturing in Kyoto, my translator Mrs. Nakatani and I set off for my father's ancestoral hometown, Hikone, aboard a "milk" train (yes they have slow trains in Japan too). Today the city is a famous tourist spot because of its location on Japan's mythical Lake Biwa and for its marvellously preserved castle. My distant relatives still live just outside Hikone, in the countryside within view of the castle.

My first familial encounter was somewhat disappointing. My

seventy-odd year old second cousin, Shig, proved to be an extremely kind and friendly man, but he was unable to point me to the Omatsu gravesite. Even with gentle prodding from Mrs. Nakatani, he was unforthcoming about my father's family, although as far as I know we are members of the same clan and our families had resided in the same hamlet for centuries.

After a tour of his spacious, slate-tiled home and following a marvellous luncheon of sushi, tempura, and baked fish, Shig led me a block down a stone-cobbled street to an abandoned house, which he identified as belonging to my family. Later that afternoon, one of Shig's daughters-in-law was summoned to take me on a tour of Hikone castle. I have a strong suspicion that given Japan's long feudal past, my relatives had been forced to toil long and hard to maintain that magnificent edifice and the indolent lifestyle of its aristocratic inhabitants. Later we took a boat ride on Lake Biwa, where according to Japanese mythology the country was founded. When we started out the sky was overcast and although it was early December the weather was mild. Just as I looked back at the castle and at the village of my father's family just beyond, the sun appeared through the clouds. There was an exotic *National Geographic* quality to the moment, with the perfect lighting, the spray of the water, and the pine trees on shore. Tears rolled down my cheeks as I regretted that my father had been unable to accompany me. Mrs. Nakatani turned to me and smiled, saying "save this moment in your heart." We returned to Kyoto later that evening.

A week later, while Frank was en route to Tokyo, I took Japan's famous bullet train from Hiroshima to Hakone, the capital city of Fukuoka, the country's southern-most island. Even in Japan, a nation that impressed me as being driven by rampant consumerism and a frenzied work ethic, I found that life in the south seemed more relaxed and informal.

The next morning I was met by my interpreter Michi, a Japanese Canadian grandmother who had been forced to return to Japan after the war with her parents. My mother's family's relatives had hired Michi's husband to drive us to Kahogun, a farming town about an hour southeast of the capital. The drive took us past fields of pale green rice paddies, tall pine forests, and craggy mountains. It reminded me of British Columbia but on a smaller, less grand scale. When my relatives landed on Canada's west coast, the similarity must have struck them as a good omen, so reminiscent of home.

We pulled up in front of a large traditional Japanese house surrounded by an exterior wall. Inside was an interior courtyard and garden. Both sides of my maternal family were gathered outside, to greet me. Ceremoniously, we exchanged bows. As tradition dictated, I presented my gifts and was then directed to a large traditional Japanese room where a huge feast had been prepared. My host, Tosh, the family patriarch, was a man in his late sixties. Strangely he reminded me of my grandfather. Both were gregarious men, continually relating stories and laughing while holding a glass of beer. Not one of my dozen or so assembled relatives spoke one word of English but we managed, with the help of Michi, my translator, to communicate.

Lunch was eaten Japanese style, sitting cross-legged on a *tatami* mat-covered floor. After a few minutes the circulation in my legs had crawled to a halt. I doubted whether I would be able to walk again. Michi had gotten into the complete swing of the party and had stopped interpreting for me. Everyone was having a good time. After examining the family albums, posing for snaps, and touring the house, we all gathered in the front hall. The trek to the family graves was next on the agenda. By now it was drizzling lightly. I was given a pair of rubber boots and we set off. We passed several rice-paddy fields and began to climb a small mountain, winding our way through bamboo groves. Suddenly in the middle of our ascent, we stopped at a clearing. There, overlooking the fields below, were two very large stone edifices, about twenty-five feet high. One tombstone belonged to my family. Tosh explained that when he died his ashes would join the ashes of five hundred of my relatives who were buried there.

At that moment, my ties to Tosh and to my ancestoral homeland felt overwhelmingly strong. I contrasted these roots to the shallow feelers we had set down on the other side of the Pacific Ocean. Now, after four generations in Canada, the entirety of my mother's family barely numbers thirty, of whom only a handful are dead. I laid the flowers and took many photographs to record the moment. We wound our way back down to the house. Before I left I visited the home of my maternal grandmother. A relative showed me a B.C. landscape scene that my grandmother had brought back to Japan in the 1930s. The oil painting was still hanging in a place of honour in the family manse to commemorate that branch who had left forever. Although intrigued about "Kanada" and their English-speaking relatives, my cousins indicated no interest in visiting. The New World, after all, was far away and very foreign.

After returning to Canada I showed inquisitive relatives my photos of our kin. Although some indicated curiosity about re-establishing ties, in the end it was concluded that the Old World is very expensive and perhaps best remembered from afar. But try as we might, Japan's presence in the lives of its transplanted offspring cannot be wished away. White racism's response to the country of my ancestors is the silent architect of our treatment in this country: the unseen navigator of our bittersweet passage. The 1980s witnessed the meteoric rise of Japan to first world status. Japan's prosperity no doubt raised suspicions about the validity of white supremacist theories that had long preached against such a possibility. Indignantly Americans found the success of a defeated enemy and former colony psychologically difficult to resolve. Relations between the two countries date back almost one hundred and fifty years, and as befits an imperialist power the United States has become accustomed to dictating orders and conditions to the Japanese. To this day it continues this foreign policy.

North American business and the press have portrayed Japan's fortunes as being at the expense of the U.S. empire. Perhaps that explains the decade of Japan bashing and scapegoating that we have witnessed. Racism is like methane gas, invisible yet always present in the low swamp lands, waiting for the spark that will set it and the countryside aflame.

Not since my youth have I felt so vulnerable because of my Japanese ancestry. Not since the 1950s have I felt so clearly an enemy alien. Today I read that seventy-five per cent of Americans regard the Japanese as their country's number one enemy. In San Francisco and Los Angeles, the Japanese American Citizens' League offices have been vandalized. History is repeating itself. Buck-teeth-grinning wartime posters have been dusted off, warning that the yellow menace is invading America and winning. Daily the growing animosity to the land of the rising sun, and thus to me, fills me with fear and apprehension. I stand helpless as the continent's racism is being manipulated to explain unemployment, deficits, and our increasing non-competitiveness. Scapegoat as enemy, my chest constricts again.

❀ | Notes

Chapter 1: The End

1. *The Toronto Star,* September 24, 1988, p.A3.
2. Escott Reid, "The Conscience of the Diplomat," *Queen's Quarterly,* quoted in Ann Sunahara, *The Politics of Racism* (Toronto: James Lorimer & Co., 1981), p.33. Pope is also quoted in Sunahara, p.33.

Chapter 2: On Being An Alien

1. Urme May Reifsnider, *Romantic History of Japan* (Tokyo: Tokyo News Service, 1953), p.i.i
2. Denny Boyd, "A Man Who Helped Shape Life Patterns," *Vancouver Sun,* June 28, 1980.

Chapter 3: Yamato-Damashii versus the Lesson of the Bamboo

1. Kazuo Ito, *Issei: A History of Japanese Immigrants in North America,* trans. S. Nakamura and J. Gerard (Seattle: Japanese Community Service, 1973), p.281.
2. Urme May Reifsnider, *Romantic History of Japan* (Tokyo: Tokyo News Service, 1953), pp.15-16.
3. Charles Young and Helen Reid, *The Japanese Canadians* (Toronto: University of Toronto Press, 1938), pp.99-102.
4. Ivan Morris, *The World of the Shining Prince* (New York: Penguin Books, 1964), p.22.
5. George Kennan, "How Japan Lost Her Chance in the Pacific," *The Outlook,* June 27, 1914, p.488.
6. See Young and Reid, p.3.
7. Jon Halliday, *A Political History of Japanese Capitalism* (New York: Pantheon Books, 1975), pp.82-84.
8. Rolf Knight and M. Koizumi, *A Man of Our Times* (Vancouver: New Star Books, 1976), p.100.
9. Pearl Buck, *The People of Japan* (New York: Simon and Schuster, 1966), p.54.
10. Young and Reid, p.xi.

11. Imre Ferenczi, "International Migration Statistics," (New York: 1929), p.160, cited in Young and Reid, p.21.

12. Adachi, Ken, *The Enemy That Never Was* (Toronto: McClelland and Stewart, 1979), p.74.

13. Sunahara, *The Politics of Racism*, p.93.

14. Adachi, p.125.

15. Quoted in Adachi, p.54.

16. Price Waterhouse, *Economic Losses to Japanese Canadians after 1941*, Vancouver, 1986, p.34.

17. Tomekichi Homma, "Looking Back," reprinted in *The New Canadian*, August 7, 1977, p.2.

18. Adachi, pp.55-62.

19. Young and Reid, p.54.

20. Ibid., p.148.

21. Rolf Knight and M. Koizumi, *A Man of Our Times* (Vancouver: New Star Books, 1976).

22. Adachi, p.48.

23. Mieko Kudo and Susan Phillips, *Vancouver no Ai* (*Love in Vancouver*),(Tokyo: Domesu Shuppau, 1982).

24. Adachi, p.29.

25. *The New Canadian*, Sept.4, 1987, p.4, reprinted from *The Fisherman*.

26. Halliday, p.82.

27. Consulate General of Japan, *Facts About Japanese in Canada and Other Miscellaneous Information*, Ottawa, 1922, pp.17-18.

28. A *biwa* is a type of four-stringed lute.

29. Lafcadio Hearn, *Kwaidan* (London: Travellers Library, 1927), p.9. For the true believer, the sought-after state of Nirvana is reached when there is an absence of consciousness of all worldly objects.

Chapter 4: War Stories

1. Muriel Kitagawa, *This Is My Own*, ed. Roy Miki (Vancouver, Talonbooks, 1985), p.216.

2. The Mackenzie quote is from the *Vancouver Province*, April 4, 1942; cited in Sunahara, p.101.

3. The Consultative Council for Cooperation in Wartime Problems of Canadian Citizenship was a Vancouver organization concerned with "real and potential abuses of Canadian citizenship in time of war." Several members of the council

had been involved in the unsuccessful attempt to gain the franchise for Japanese Canadians in 1936. Key members of the council were Rev. Howard Norman, president, and Dr. Henry Angus of the Department of External Affairs. Cited in Sunahara, p.191.

4. Adachi, pp.333-334.

5. *Iwasaki v. Queen* (1969) 1 Ex. C.R. 281, Affirmed (1970) S.C.R. 437. The Court declared that the property held by the Custodian was not held in trust but was his; thus he could do with it as he wished.

6. Sunahara, p.114.

7. The categories to be deported were: all Japanese aliens who had signed for repatriation or who had been interned at Angler; all naturalized Japanese Canadians and all Canadian-born Japanese who had not revoked their repatriation requests; and the wives and minors of all of these groups.

8. Quoted in Sunahara, p.144.

9. Adachi, p.310.

10. *Reference re the Validity of Orders-in-Council of Dec. 15, 1945 (PC 7355, 56, 57)* re Persons of the Japanese Race (1945) S.C.R. 248; Affirmed *Co-operative Committee on JCs v. AG-of Can.* (1947) A.C. 87 (P.C.).

11. Of these, 34 per cent were Japanese aliens, 15 per cent naturalized Japanese Canadians, and 51 per cent Canadian-born. Over 1,300 of the repatriates and most of the Canadian-born were children under the age of sixteen. Canada, Department of Labour, "Report on the Re-establishment of Japanese in Canada, 1944-46," p.15, quoted in Sunahara, p.197.

12. Sunahara, pp.144-145.

13. Judge Patel, re *Korematsu* decision, as quoted in William Hohri, *Repairing America: An Account of the Movement for JA Redress*, (Pullman, Wa.:Washington State University Press, 1988), p.196.

14. *The New Canadian*, August 23, 1947; quoted in Adachi, p.342.

15. The New Canadian (Toronto), June 7, 1947, quoted in Adachi, pp.340-341.

16. Sachimaro Moro-oka, *Arusu Sensen E (At the Battle of Arras)* (Tokyo: Gunjin Kaikan Jig-yo-bu, 1935), cited in Roy Ito, *We Went to War* (Stittsville, Ont.: Canada's Wings, 1984), p.57.

17. Adachi, p.343.

18. Ibid.

19. Nakano, *Within the Barbed Wire Fence* (Toronto: University of Toronto Press, 1980), pp.66, 93-94.

Chapter 5: The Tide Turns

1. Kitagawa, p.216.
2. They included men such as Kunio Hidaka, a Toronto redress activist responsible for encouraging his niece, Professor Audrey Kobayashi, to become a Montreal representative, and community stalwart Roger Obata.
3. Tom Shoyama, "Redress and the War Time Years," *The New Canadian*, Vol.49, No.4 (January 18, 1985), pp.1-2.
4. *The Globe and Mail*, July 30, 1982.
5. *The Globe and Mail*, Oct. 12, 1983.
6. *The Gazette* (Montreal), Jan. 27, 1984, Editorial, p.B2.
7. *The Toronto Sun*, April 5, 1984, Editorial p.10.
8. *The Globe and Mail*, Editorial, April 4, 1984.
9. Hansard, Debates of the Senate, 2nd session, 32nd Parliament, Vol. 129, no. 33, May 8, 1984, pp.522, 531.
10. *The Toronto Star*, June 19, 1984.
11. Members of the NAJC strategy team from 1984 to 1988 were: President Art Miki, Roy Inouye (Kamloops), Bryce Kanbara (Hamilton), Audrey Kobayashi (Montreal), Cassandra Kobayashi (Vancouver), Roy Miki (Vancouver), Roger Obata (Toronto), Maryka Omatsu (Toronto).
12. *The Globe and Mail*, Sept. 14, 1983.
13. Original members were: writers Joy Kogawa and Frank Moritsugu, lawyers Marcia Matsui, Shin Imai, Connie Sugiyama and Maryka Omatsu, and civil servant Ron Shimizu.
14. *The New Canadian*, April 26, 1985, p.1.
15. Some of the members of the Toronto chapter were: Van Hori, Shirley Yamada, Bill and Addie Kobayashi, Yuki Mizuyabu, Matt Matsui, Wes and Misao Fujiwara, Stan Hiraki, Yo Mori, Ken Noma, Blanche Hyodo, Dennis Madokoro, Susan Hidaka, and Harry Yonekura.
16. *The Globe and Mail*, June 2, 1986.

Chapter 6: Legal Pawns of Fate

1. Jack Scott, "The Crime of Being Born," *Vancouver Sun*, October 30, 1948; quoted in Adachi, p.338.
2. Adachi, pp.337-338.
3. In particular, the NAJC brief made the following recommendations: 1) that the Constitution be amended to include a clause specifically protecting the rights of racial and ethnic minorities similar to section 28, which safeguarded only the

rights of women; 2) that section 15 be strengthened, by preventing governments from overriding or opting out of the Charter's equality rights provisions; and 3) that a clause be added requiring the payment of redress for any abrogation of rights.

4. Letter from Beatty to Miki, May 5, 1988.
5. Letter from Miki to Beatty, May 25, 1988.
6. The amendment would read something like this, in section 28(2): "Notwithstanding anything in this Charter, except for provisions 15(2) and 25, the rights and freedoms referred to in it are guaranteed equally to all persons regardless of their ethnicity, race, colour or religion."
7. Recommendations of *Personal Justice Denied: Report of the Commission on Wartime Relocation and Internment of Civilians*, Part II, Washington, D.C., 1983, p. 5.
8. Ibid, pp. 8-10.
9. Letter from Roman to Omatsu, May 1, 1985.
10. William Hohri, *Repairing America* (Pullman, Wa.: Washington State University Press, 1988), p.191.
11. Ibid. p. 205.

Chapter 7: In the Corridors of Power: 1984-88

1. Miyamota Musashi, *The Book of Five Rings* (New York: Bantam, 1982), p.72.
2. John Fraser, M.P., "Minutes of the Proceedings and Evidence of the Special Joint Committee of the Senate and of the House of Commons on the Constitution of Canada," November 26, 1980.
3. *The Globe and Mail,* February 2, 1985.
4. Ibid.
5. *The Globe and Mail,* January 28, 1986.
6. *The Globe and Mail,* editorial, March 8, 1986.
7. Hansard, May 14, 1986, p.13268.
8. Hansard, June 3, 1986.
9. Hansard, May 28, 1986, p.13718.
10. *The Globe and Mail,* July 1, 1986.
11. *The Ottawa Citizen,* Dec.9, 1986.
12. *The Globe and Mail,* February 2, 1985.
13. Judy Steed, *Pursuit of Power* (Toronto: Penguin Books, 1988), p.81.
14. For instance, see *The Toronto Star,* April 17, 1988.

Chapter 8: Taking It to the People

1. *The Lethbridge Herald*, editorial, April 15, 1985.
2. Ibid.
3. *The Globe and Mail*, April 29, 1985.
4. *Personal Justice Denied: Report of the Commission on Wartime Relocation and Internment of Civilians* (Washington, D.C., 1982), p.258.
5. Canada, House of Commons, *Equality Now: Participation of Visible Minorities in Canadian Society* (Ottawa, 1984), recommendations 33 and 34.
6. *Mennonite Brethren Herald*, Vol.23, No.15, July 27, 1984, p.12.

Chapter 9: Glass Ball Reflections

1. *Shizuo Endo, Kabasan jiken*, Tokyo, 1971, p.264, cited in Bowen, Roger, *Rebellion and Democracy in Meiji Japan* (Berkeley, Ca.: University of California Press, 1980), p.1.
2. Bowen, p.1.
3. Ibid, p.72.
4. Ibid, p.117.
5. Peter Worthington, "This Election Promise Should Be Kept," *Financial Post*, August 15, 1988, p.15.
6. Andrew Nikiforuk and Edward Struzik, "The Great Forest Sell-Off," *The Globe and Mail Report on Business Magazine*, November 1989, pp.62-63.
7. *Maclean's*, February 19, 1990, p.35.
8. William Purves, *The Globe and Mail*, March 3, 1990.
9. Ramsay Cook letter to David Crombie, reprinted in *The New Canadian*, Spring 1987.
10. Maryka Omatsu, "Canadian Japanese Doubt Charter's Safeguards," *The Globe and Mail*, July 20, 1984.
11. Order-in-Council P.C. 1988-89/2552.

❀ | Index